the pressures of addiction

finding a way out

S.R. MAYS

S.H.E. PUBLISHING, LLC

PRESSURES OF ADDICTION

Copyright © 2024 by S.R. Mays

For information contact:

www.shepublishingllc.com | info@shepublishingllc.com

Cover and Title Page Design by Michelle Phillips of CHELLD3 3D VISUALIZATION AND DESIGN

ISBN: 978-1-964061-08-5

First Edition: June 2024

10 9 8 7 6 5 4 3 2 1

FOREWORD

A brother, father, son, and friend are how he is seen. But the author, "S.R. Mays," of this book is also an inspiration to so many. To inspire takes courage, and courageousness is all part of your DNA. Your meekness stretches far and wide. To watch you transition from a dark space into the light brought joy to my heart because so many people who are in that darkness yearn to see their light. You allowed your spiritual man to rule over the flesh. Just know God is pleased. Anyone who picks up this book to read or any other book you have written or will write will be able to understand or even find themselves in one or more of the situations you have been through. You are a walking testimony and a beacon of hope, so continue to hold on to your faith and inspire others to hold on to theirs.

Love always, **Sis Shenikia Jett**

CONTENTS

INTRODUCTION

This book will give you details of my struggles with substance abuse. It will also give details of the challenges I faced in my efforts to address the problem. Then it will point out the moment my purpose went from overcoming my demons to attempting to help others who are struggling.

By bringing attention to the impact substances have on abusers, their family, and friends and by identifying the dangers- seen and unseen- It may be possible to encourage, influence, or even scare those who want to seek help but do not yet know how to go about taking the first step. *Through my pain, I sought help from the "Source of all Creation."*

A lot of abusers are in truth, the ones being abused. Abusing drugs, or another person is a sign of demonic possession. Demons abuse everyone they possess. *There are no demons of peace and joy, they come to steal, kill, and destroy.* Identifying them and addressing them can bring an abuser closer to taking that first step.

In my struggles, prayer helped me recognize and understand what I needed to do. I understood that there was a process, and that process would require patience. In the early chapters of this book, the reader will see how much of a challenge it would be to practice patience.

Because of the persistent cry for help through prayers, listening for an answer, having the solution to my prayers presented before me, and then showing my gratitude by taking the appropriate actions, I was delivered from the demonic possession of addiction.

I was delivered by grace, and I want others to know that they can be delivered as well. I have no doubt that the act of obedience provided cover for me by the Holy Spirit throughout the entire recovery process.

Always start any journey with prayer and supplication.

■■■

Outlining The Process: Preparing for Recovery

A journey starts with the first step. Recovering from abuse is a journey that requires the abuser to complete a process. For my journey I needed to prepare for that first step.

Keeping a journal was something I have no explanation for doing. At the time, it was done to pass time. I cannot say I was inspired to write my thoughts and feelings, but as I kept doing it, I became driven to do so-unfortunately, the journals I shared in this book were just a fraction of what I originally had. Many of the original pages were lost.

Documenting my thoughts and feelings while under the influence of my drug of choice, (heroin), provided a way for me to feel like I was accomplishing something useful. Even though I had no idea how it would be used, I continued to write. Being under this influence was the only time I had the mental energy to physically function. My prime writing periods were immediately after taking that first "hit," especially when it had been some days between the last time I had used. My journaling turned out to be a key step on the road to recovery and the basis on which this book is written.

As I continued to write I could look back on previous notes and see how bad life had gotten for me. The documentation from 2002 through 2007 at the beginning of this book reveals the struggles I experienced. The more I wrote and reviewed the previous notes, the more I began to desire to be free from the struggle.

The entire act of journaling was preparing me to begin the journey to end my addiction. What this act did was:

• Develop the desire to seek change in my life.

• Develop the willpower to change my life.

• Build up the courage to begin the pursuit of a better life.

• Find the right path to recovery. For me it was a clinical treatment program.

• Gave me the mindset and the patience to do whatever it takes to complete the process.

What I have outlined is the process that worked for me, - which I have detailed in this book. The important thing to understand is that recovery will require some type of process. Unknowingly, what began that process for me was journaling.

Going back and looking at logs from the days or weeks prior, revealed how I was struggling to combat the disease of addiction alone during that period. Slowly I began to realize that I needed to find help.

The journals were a reference to my past and current struggles during that time. They also became a catalyst for my desire to seek outside help. That desire became the first of the five steps I noted.

■■■

Life After Recovery: The Process Continues

The purpose of this book is to encourage those who struggle with not just substance abuse but any abuse. By sharing my journey, I hope to do my part to help others who struggle with substance abuse, since this was my struggle as well.

I stated earlier that at the time I had no explanations for why I kept a journal. During and after my treatment I had not thought about them. Twelve years later I discovered them in an old binder where I had stored them. I had been carrying them from apartment to apartment, but I had not read them until then. After reading these documents again with a changed perspective I finally received an explanation to why I wrote them many years ago. There was a divine purpose involved.

As I was reading them, the first thing I recognized that I had not recognized before was that abuse of any kind is a form of demonic possession.

Overcoming addiction is a form of being reborn. My rebirth allowed me to view things differently and with more clarity. It was as if my spiritual nature had been re-awakened. My interest in the supernatural had grown since I had been treated for my addiction. I began to see people not just as flesh and blood individuals, but as vessels for spirits to occupy as well. Looking back over my journals I could see how an evil spirit had taken control of my life and that I was powerless to overcome it.

With my supernatural spirit being awakened, it became clear that I had to share my revelations from this experience with others who may be struggling with addiction. This book is my second attempt to do so-look for the first one called **"The Effective use of Spiritual Tools"** by S. R. Mays in paperback.

At the time I wrote these journals I could not have imagined my perspective would change the way it has. Nor did I recognize the numerous revelations it contained. As I look back and consider that these journals were written while I was under the influence of drugs, I am convinced that a supernatural force was in control of my thoughts and guiding my writing hand. These journals became a beacon of light that originated and later emanated from a dark place.

The reason journaling is important is because it documents various stages of the struggle. It is also important to include the reactions of family and friends, those who were supportive and the ones who were not. You might view their actions and reactions much differently after your rebirth.

To this day I continue to bring awareness to the consequences of abuse and encourage abusers to seek help.

That is why I have written two books and hosted my own podcast on You Tube called **"Overcoming Addiction"** by Sandy R. Mays.

I will not mislead anyone to believe that life after recovery is an easy one. It is still life, and it will always have difficulties. What I do support is the idea that even during difficulties, a sober person will always be better able to cope with the challenges than one who is battling with demons.

I hope whoever reads this and my first book will consider sharing some of the insights I have shared.

The pain and the struggles I endured in the past fuel my purpose for today and beyond.

CHAPTER I

In these next few pages, I am going to share my thoughts and feelings as I struggled with addiction. These notes are from journals that I kept during that time. It is not a daily diary as you will notice by the huge gaps in the dates. But it will give the reader an idea of how I struggled with the demons of addiction. Again, these are just thoughts that indicated the struggles I had with addiction. There is no beginning to the story or end to the story, in fact, in these pages, it is about the struggle that went on over years. Most of the time I did write some of my feelings down, but a lot of them were not put in writing. The ones I did write down are being shared in this book.

I should also include that over this five-year period is when I began to come to the realization that it was time for me to decide if I wanted to fight for change in my life or accept the path I was on. Without realizing it at the time, some other force was guiding me. I began to accept exactly what I had become. I did not understand at the time why I was suddenly compelled to admit I was an addict.

This entire period is when I cried out the most. More so than I had ever cried out before or have since. Looking back, it seems as though at that time I was preparing myself -or just building up my courage, to take the initial steps of laying the foundation for my recovery process. I guess it could be called a five-year groundbreaking cry for help.

■■

Acceptance

August 18th. 2002.

There are many things that I have some understanding of. And there are just as many things that I have little knowledge of. Also, there are a lot of things which I know absolutely nothing about. But there is one thing which I am very sure of, and that is how to be a substance abuser. In fact, I have so much knowledge of this subject I have earned an MDA degree on the subject. MDA simply means, "Major Drug Addict." And this degree only indicates how much of a nobody its bearer really is. Those of us who have earned it can spend the rest of our lives trying to rid ourselves of such a degrading award. A person must really, really want to be free from an addiction of any kind, and there are ways to do so.

Of course, there are mainstream methods for treating substance abuse, such as medical treatment facilities. But even with the mainstream methods, if the individual has no serious deep-down desire to quit, often, fail. A proven alternative method is to seek the help of the Heavenly Father. And in doing so, you will receive the guidance necessary to successfully conquer the devil's influence, which is why it has been difficult to succeed in the past for me. It is the devil who can cause you to see pleasure when using drugs, instead of the real destruction taking place with your mind and body. The only way to defeat his influence is to develop and maintain a strong relationship with God. Once you have made the first step and you are sincere, God will show you what you need to do. Next, it is especially important that you have faith. Not a little faith but a lot of faith. Your faith must be unbending. This faith along with strong commitment and determination will bring about the necessary changes in attitude which must accompany the will to end any type of abuse or social misbehavior.

It would be nine years later before I was able to take this first step.

■■■

Misuse Leads to Abuse

August 21st, 2002.

During the time I was a slave to narcotics, whenever my mother and I had an argument, no matter what my response or how I responded, she would always say that it is the drugs talking. If I sounded excited, it was the drugs. If I disagree, it was the drugs. Even when I said nothing, it was the drugs. Whatever my response, it was the drugs. As I thought about those arguments for weeks I concluded. That the next time we argue, I would agree with her. And just as she started, her favorite phrase. I would jump in and say, you know mom, you are right, drugs do talk. But they only say one thing. They say that if you abuse me, I will kill you. That is, it. Nothing else. I do not have to tell you what her response was the next time I did this. Especially after I wanted to know how it is that someone who has never used drugs can always hear it talking. I told her in truth, according to her, all drugs, including aspirins, say the same thing, which is if you abuse me, I will kill you. My point is, it is not only about the drug, but also about the misuse of it or anything else. If any person claims to hear drugs talking, they should look at themselves and seek professional help. Also, seek more information about drug abuse. Take the time to find out how much the disease affects people. Not only the user, but people around them. Find ways to assist with treatments, be supportive and along with patients, have faith. Outside support, no matter how much, can help. Most addicts struggle with their addiction. And outside support can ease the struggle. If this is too much to give, then the next best option is to just shut up. Criticism creates hostility. anger and overall become dangerous.

In case you could not figure out my mother's response, it was "that's the drugs talking."

∎∎∎

Denial and Hypocrisy

August 22nd. 2002.

It serves no purpose whatsoever for a person infected with any type of disease, or deficiency such as alcohol or a controlled substance to continue to convince themselves that their dependency can be easily overcome. To do so requires a sincere effort to first change one's attitude. You must take a firm stance against that "I need something so I can do whatever" attitude. You must seek God's help to develop willpower. If you take the initial steps along the way, he will strengthen your will to do whatever it takes to overcome. You must develop and maintain a desire to overcome. With God's help that desire will be strengthened. You must have faith in God's wisdom. For he knows in advance what the outcome will be. Depending upon the path you decide to travel. What road we choose to travel is our decision and ours alone. And the more we understand the consequences of our decisions, the greater our chances of making a wiser decision. Doing what we know is wrong and having others believe that we are righteous, is being in a hypocritical state of mind? You are denying yourself the chance to receive any wisdom from God himself. Again, the decision is ours to make.

I knew all this then but did not have the courage at the time to act on these wise observations of mine.

■ ■

Attempt at Freedom

September 7th. 2002.

I would like to try and describe what I experienced as I tried to free myself one time of substance abuse on my own.

Taking any kind of mind and or body altering substance is like riding in a locomotive. You start off slow, wanting only to take a short trip at a slow speed which you think is safe and enjoyable. And it is enjoyable. You tell yourself that if you ride along at this slow speed, you can stop the ride at any time and get off until the next time. Before you know you are riding more. Next thing you know, the train is going faster.

One day you decide to get off this train, but now it is traveling so fast that if you jump off, you might hurt yourself. So, you say, well, let me slow this thing down to a safe speed and then jump off. But by this time the train was moving so fast that it had left the ground. In fact, it is not even a train anymore. You are now cruising in a Starship traveling at warp speed. And you are now the captain.

Now you are asking yourself, how and when did this happen and how do I get off this thing without killing myself? So, you start to fear, and the only thing to do is hope that someday you wake up and find that this is only a dream. But it is a nightmare.

Here is how I managed to find my way back on this occasion.

After realizing that it is up to me and me alone to end this ride, I concluded that I first had to return to Earth because at warp speed, I had traveled way beyond this solar system. It seemed an impossible task which felt like it would take the rest of my life. But if this is what I had to do then so be it.

It was a rough ride, but somehow, I made it back to Earth. Now I had to get off the Starship, which I did. But I wound up on a jet plane. I did not give up. With determination and patience, I found myself back aboard that train. Still, it was moving at an extremely high speed. Too fast for me to jump off. Safely. I still had to slow it down.

It took a lot of willpower to continue this reverse journey. But by remaining diligent I was able to slow it down enough where I could safely get off.

Once I got off the most horrible ride of my life, I discovered there is a tougher task ahead. That is staying off.

I could not stay off the ride.

■■■

The War Begins

October 1st, 2002.

What I would like to do in this essay is to try and convey what it is like to be involved with this war on substance abuse, which I have been undertaking virtually alone. There are many types of battle that must be won to claim victory in this war. Some outsiders who never have been in this position will label my strategy as running from the problem one has been fighting and losing one battle after another. The wise move and my mind would be to retreat, regroup, reassess, and reorganize yourself before reengaging the enemy. There are times to attack, and there are times when one should defend. It is better to attack, with solid persistence which you can only have with careful planning and determination. When you have spent 25 years at war and losing more individual battles then you win. You start to wonder if you will ever be capable of winning the war before time runs out. Yet. This is a war that must be won, and not be decided via the ultimate and inevitable outcome known as death. I must point out that over the years during the many battles, a person's body physically takes a beating, leaving one drained and without the drive needed to withstand the continuous pains of withdrawal that accompany that act of retreating. Also, while overcoming this physical condition, you can become mentally drained. And depending upon how long your war has been going on, it may require a lengthy period before any relief is recognized. What you must do is first be persistent. Second, be patient. And most important, third, have faith in God. First, the rewards may be small and subtle, which is why you must be persistent. Relief may take a while to be noticed. You must have patience, and if you are determined and dedicated, your faith will gradually grow. Faith is the single most important quality which will guide you through any adverse situation, substance abuse notwithstanding. Without it, success is a foregone failure, as in any conflict. Once you regroup and prepare to do battle again, prayer and faith will become your most powerful tools. In time, after numerous attempts, your body begins to readjust to functioning without substance. Once this process begins, you will need to keep yourself properly nourished to allow your body to heal from the damage Caused by years of neglect. Because of this some body functions do not function as they should. But the body can repair itself, given time.

Next comes the more complicated task of mentally purging yourself of the demon. This I consider to be the hardest to overcome because your brain is deprived of a chemical which it has become dependent upon. Also, the routines which accompany substance abuse are hard to change. When your brain becomes accustomed to the routine of wanting it, then acquiring it, and then enjoying the results of the process over and over, day by day. week by week. It becomes a hard habit to break. You must gradually change this routine and usually the first step is the most important. This is not an overnight procedure and there may be setbacks. This is why you must persist. Be patient, stay determined, and again maintain faith in the Almighty. I believe I will overcome it.

Understanding how drug abuse affects us biologically as well was my way of arming myself with a tool which I thought would be helpful. Information.

■■■

Being Supportive

October 2nd, 2002.

The value of being supportive to a person with any kind of affliction is only measured by the kindness and appreciation felt by the one in need of it. There can be many ways support can benefit an ailing individual. It may also be given to various degrees. However, when it is presented, it must be done without self-serving reasons, and any type of support should be accepted. The person suffering goes through periods of depression and fear. Of failure, hopelessness, and dejection. The value of something as simple as listening to a recovering addict cannot be measured. A lot of times people think that giving advice, offering solutions and even criticizing is being supported. Most of the abusers already know what needs to be done to correct the problem. Even constructive criticism can have the opposite effect. What is needed is reassurance. And or a quiet listening ear. This is a very tough task for someone who has never had a substance abuse problem. For those people, the problem does not resemble a disease, which it is. I have been accused of seeking support as a means of securing sympathy and pity. I feel that these traits do not aid in recovery. When a person is being supportive, it should be done deep down, honestly, sincerely, and with consideration. Or not be done at all. Sometimes the effects are subtle, and other times being supportive will have a profound impact, however, it is felt. If its results are positive, the road to recovery may just be a little easier.

Support from someone who has gone through a recovery process resonates more with an addict than from someone who not only has not gone through the process but has never used drugs.

■■

Compassion

October 4th, 2002

The dictionary defines compassion as the feeling of sorrow for the suffering of others. Being compassionate is showing kindness. Tenderness and sympathy. For people recovering from substance abuse, the need for compassion is about as important as showing it. The reasons being. People who have never had a substance problem believe it is something a person willingly inflicts upon themselves. The truth is. There is no way of knowing in advance how much of an effect. And to what degree and especially the agony and misery felt when your mind and body becomes separated from the substance for a period. Although I can tell people what it is like. Unless they have had that experience, it would be impossible for anyone to understand.

Addiction is a disease, and like any other disease, there are symptoms. Some obvious, some not so obvious. But uneducated individuals who will accept something like cancer, or aids as a disease, would be unable to accept addiction as one. Thus, they are incapable of being compassionate. For some reason they feel that anyone afflicted with an addiction does not deserve compassion. Something I have noticed is that if you ask them why they do not show compassion, you will not receive a substantial answer. In fact. They are going to think you do not deserve a response. When I decided to travel the road to recovery, I knew it would be a long journey. So, I packed myself a mental suitcase. And in this suitcase, I packed all the emotions I felt I would need on this long trip. I packed patients. Understanding. Dedication. Humility. Compassion. And most of all, faith. All these emotions, along with some other items, turned out to be quite necessary. Also, I have discovered a means of detecting honest and sincere compassionate individuals from those who will have you to believe they are compassionate.

Compassion is something that should be given unconditionally. It is what God has installed in everyone, though some do not know how to use it. A person fighting with the influences of substance abuse has a greater need. Some are not aware that it is a fight for life. And not. A fight for a lifestyle.

Those who have never had an addiction of any kind believe that the disease of addiction is something addicts choose to continue to indulge in out of joy.

Confusion

December 26. 2005.

On November the 25th in 2005, I began a journey. And like any other, it started with the first step, this journey would begin with the hope of overcoming restrictions, limitations, setbacks, mentally and physically. Satan uses fear in these areas to ensure his success. So, to take the first step, there must be a clear understanding of what it will produce and how to make it a productive one. In my case, the first step was to overcome my fears, which were a byproduct of my own demons. Little did I know that recognizing my demons to overcome the fears manifested by the demons would require a vast amount of time that would be no less than three to four months, (for an addict that seems like forever). That is just to take the first step.

I had to come to the realization that not only would this step involve willpower, dedication, and intestinal fortitude. But I would have to accomplish it alone. Just the thought of this added to the fears. I had to be absolutely, completely committed just to taking the first step, knowing my journey may take me three to four months before I had enough necessities to physically meet the challenge of living a drug-free life. Overcoming my fear would become spiritually, emotionally, and mentally, the most monumental task I have ever undertaken at this point in my life. And again, I would have to do it alone.

When you use drugs for as long as I had "over 25 years at this point", to tell yourself that you are one day going to just stop overnight is unrealistic. It is as unrealistic as saying to yourself that you were never an addict. It is like leaving a 30-year marriage, that, on the surface, made you quite content if not happy at times. But deep down it was not only disabling, but resulted in only one sure outcome, the end of my life. I never felt the addiction was severe enough where I would overdose. My fear was being afflicted with something and not being aware until it was too late. The drug gives you a false sense of being sound and seeming to be healthy. The drug has the tendency of masking or neutralizing warning symptoms and signs that the body manufacturers to indicate when and where there are problems. Physically as well as mentally. I am talking about strokes, heart attacks, blood clots, etc. Many things can be treated if there is nothing compromising the body's warning system. Now one would think, wow, now I know what the consequences of using heroin are and stopping is going to be a snap.

To continue using is suicide. To continue in this marriage will lead to my death. But how do you just walk away from something you have relied upon for so long that has gotten you through a lot of tough, stressful, unhappy times? This is what being dependent encompasses. Now you depend on your drug for everything. Whatever I needed to do, I could not do until I fulfilled what started as something I wanted to feel good. It became a need which I believe provided me with confidence and, more importantly, the physical drive which I would not have if I did not have the drug. I am attempting to break down the many, many small steps involved which are essential in making the initial step. The reality is, once it has been made, you may find yourself looking up and seeing your goals so far away and it may seem as though you will never reach them because of the effort and time it would take, not to mention having to do so with no outside help. Looking for progress can be compared to watching grass grow in slow motion. Combine this process with the reality of slip ups and setbacks and the amount of determination and willpower will dictate success or failure. And even so, a helping hand would have been welcome. When there is nothing forthcoming, you do what you must do to keep your focus. Seek small victories. You will not win every battle, especially at first. When you do lose, you have to regroup, revise and not allow small setbacks to determine overall success and failure remember, I have many years of dependency and if I have to first break this part, the next phase is continuing to retrain the part of my brain that feels the rest of me has to have this drug in order to function. Breaking the dependency is just one of the necessary and crucial components which go into that first tiny yet major step. In fact, it is the most significant task to be overcome and maintained. For me, this task, once achieved, will require constant attention throughout the remainder of my life. It is an area which I will forever need reinforcements. That first step of overcoming fear is the beginning of the slow climb and the area which requires a strengthening of the foundation I need for me to have any hope of defeating this illness. Up to this point I find myself still doing this initial step. I discovered that there is no road map, no information desk and, especially for me, no understanding as to what lies down the road. I do not believe there is one formula which will apply to everyone. Even if everyone suffered from the same addiction or illness. At this point, it is not just day-to-day. But moment to moment. I find myself experiencing moments of complete control as well as moments of uncertainty. It truly is frustrating to look back over 30 days (about 4 and a half weeks) and feel as though I am making no progress at all. This for me is an area where I have not been for some time. To be able to just have an appetite, be able to watch television, just a few of many trivial things that I would not or could not do, due to chemical dependency. For me, these small achievements mean more than words can describe. They gave me a taste of a lifestyle for which I longed. It has only been 30 days (about 4 and a half weeks), and still, the first step has yet to be completed. And I must admit, I fear my frustration may lead to depression. Then into desperation. And since this is an area where I have not been for quite some time, I do believe there will be another confrontation. These are things that I will face alone. The choices are mine, and the desire to overcome the next challenges strengthens my foundation. Therein lies the motivation. If I do not allow fear to scare me away from a confrontation which may or may not occur, I can maintain my focus, and strengthen my resolve. I will do what I must do. It is extremely difficult to describe the magnitude of the task and path I have undertaken. And even if there are setbacks, I cannot return to a life of complete dependency.... to be continued.

■■■

January 6, 2006.

The temptation is not as severe now as it used to be a couple of months ago. And by the grace of God, and through his guidance. I can see a little more clearly the benefits of willpower, Faith. and determination. Still, discipline and commitment have become attributes which I have yet to conquer. But since this will be a lengthy process. My position now is far better than two months ago. Every day I search for a mechanism I can routinely use to nullify sudden urges. Now that my body does not need to be sustained artificially by something unhealthy. My mind is free to search for solutions and devise permanent resolutions. Giving me restitution. And complete control of my willpower. This is an attribute everyone should aspire to have as well. Determination. Discipline. Commitment. And the all-important addition of faith. Tomorrow, God's will, I will again attempt to make another day, and because

I want to live a healthy life, I will continue my search for an effective technique that will allow me to corral this oppressor. And then destroy it forever.

■■■

March 3rd, 2006.

To just say curiosity has gotten the best of me would grossly understate the accuracy of my predicament. Now the thing which I have dreaded all along has presented itself. My honesty compels me to admit to this setback. But my desire to overcome it hopefully will not allow it to become a substantial illness in a manner which had relentlessly consumed me for so long. I have decided not to dwell upon the situation but instead concentrate on my successful accomplishments. I just need to satisfy these infrequent urges to answer the questions I have asked myself.

As the days become weeks. I had often wondered what would become of me if I just did it once. I wonder if I had enough willpower built up to be able to do so and walk away, and not have the urge to continue to indulge myself.

This document is now being drafted incomplete. At this time, I do not know for sure if I can resist. At this moment, for the sake of sincerity, I will make every effort to return to my desired chosen path, which is a path to freedom. Freedom of my mind. Body and soul. Where failure is not an option.

■■■

March the 7th. 2006.

Which means I have been under the influence since the 3rd of this month. I can feel my willpower diminishing, and I fear that along with this fear, my determination has also weakened. Also, the physical discomfort which accompanies the abuse has begun to manifest itself. I must find a way to disperse these feelings because I do not want to become a slave to this addiction ever again. The following day is when I must reapply the effort. I will have to start at the beginning, just like the previous days, weeks, and months. It seems as if all those efforts were for nothing. I just hope to be able to restore a small amount of willpower that I gained over that period and pray it is sufficient to place me back on the proper path, with just enough drive and determination to overcome this unpleasant and unwanted setback.

I make no excuses. Nobody is perfect. All this is just part of the process. My failure is simply due to having no sense of commitment and no willpower. I can only hope and pray that this does not ever occur again.

My fear fueled my confusion. From December of 2006 to March 2007 every time I had a little success, the fear of failing would eventually win out. I did not know if this back and forth was for better or worse.

■■

Starting to Weaken

March 23rd, 2006.

At this point in time, I do not have the slightest clue of what I am doing. I am discovering that due to the extensive amount of abuse for the extended length of time I spent abusing, the task of rehabilitating has proven to be a much, much larger process than I had hoped it would be. I thought that I had an idea of the length, but there is a long, lengthy process. Which at the same time, presents peaks and valleys that require an enormous amount of willpower. From the moment I awakened until the time I went to bed.

I had no idea that it would still be this difficult. Although my body has overcome its dependency, my brain still cannot seem to adjust to life without having to have some kind of stimulation. And since it was so dependent for such an extended period on a substance that is the most addictive narcotic there is, I am beginning to realize just how weak my willpower is and how powerful my foe is.

I produced this strategy to hopefully assist me with combatting my addiction. It only consists of me documenting my thoughts. The impact of a spoken word can be measured by the degree of how it is perceived once it has been received. Any addict with any real talent will find it difficult for their abilities to fully be applied, especially if their habit is being fully supplied. Supplying the habit prevents the potential from fully being achieved. Drawbacks will manifest themselves both mentally and physically. The purpose of this document is to help bring me to the point where I can gradually reduce my dependency so I can make the first leap without harming myself.

Here I am hoping to find strength by recognizing my weakness.

··

Calling Out

April 9th. 2006.

It is quite clear that, despite what I consider to be my most intense attempt, to this point, to overcome this addiction. I realized I will not be able to overcome this disease unless I seek outside treatments. Over the last five months, my willpower and determination have not been what I desired. There have been difficulties. And periods of weakness. This inconsistency has caused more depression, something I have tried to prevent, because when I am depressed, I lose hope. Another condition I try to avoid is stress. But with the depression I now have two illnesses to deal with. Now knowing I must combat harder adds stress; therefore, I am battling 3 very controlling conditions. Having to maintain my willpower while attempting to deal with depression, and attempting to avoid stress is something I did not perceive to be as difficult as it now has become. Initially I was prepared to confront these symptoms individually. I now have learned that because I abuse my mind and body for an exceedingly long time, no matter how hard and how much I am able to refrain from this addiction. I am not equipped with some very vital tools that are crucial if I am to recover.

I do not just want to stop using drugs. My desire is to recover my mind, body, and soul. I have also realized how important it is to have outside support. Outside, as in family and or friends. I also can understand better the importance of group support. As in receiving treatment away from situations that may allow the opportunities to experience the moments of weakness that may occur. From my previous experiences, (I tried a 28-day program in 1989 and failed), being with a group of people whose primary goals are all the same, is a distinctive style of support. One that provides a sense of security, and helps develop a firm foundation which, once you establish, you can start to build upon it. This strengthens your mental resolve, thus increasing willpower while creating, then extending the distance between that period of addiction and the period of recovery. The greater the distance, the stronger your willpower will become. The stronger your willpower becomes, the easier it gets to abstain. The more you abstain, the better your spirits are. The better your spirits are, the less stress. Avoid the pressure caused by the constant battle, and that becomes the area that will not cause depression. All these things and symptoms must be addressed and overcome to increase the chances of a healthy, happy fulfilled remainder of life.

■■

April the 24th, 2006.

Despite my most sincere attempts. Overcoming all the many effects substance abuse produces. Using my current method is leaving me disappointed, to say the least. At this exact moment I feel like crying. In fact, I do cry. Still, it does no good. There have been changes, both physical and mental. But they are so minute. I feel more frustration than progress. My desire has been altered. My need has been diminished slightly. My desire to change lacks motivation.

In fact, my motivation is becoming increasingly less a natural inclination and more of something that needs to be manufactured. Overcoming this challenge remains my heart's most desire. I just cannot seem to find the courage to reach out for fear of not finding complete satisfaction. My one fear right now is not being able to be patient enough to apply for treatment. Which can take months sometimes. It can take months just to be interviewed. And then there is the waiting for an opening which can take who knows how long. Now for someone in need of instant help, red tape can discourage one very easily. For me, the last thing I wanted to hear is. Call us every week to see if we have rooms available. It makes things more difficult on top of current feelings of worthlessness. I do not understand how there can be so few treatment programs for an illness that if not treated instantly, can and will lead to death and destruction. There is suicide for those who cannot cope. Murder for those who do so to support their addiction, along with burglary, robbery and many other crimes which can be avoided. I realized that there are many addicts in line for treatment centers. But in our society, a society that produces all types of prosperity, it would appear to me to be something that can be solved. Once an addict is treated successfully, another experienced counselor is created. It is just impossible not to have enough people to manage and run treatment programs. Having facilities should be the easiest obstacle to overcome. Federal and state programs are in place already to aid with facilities such as housing, which can be converted into treatment centers. My frustration is growing. I need divine intervention. All the way in every way, even though I can feel the slight change. But I am looking for more of a solid impact regarding change. But it is so faint and moves along at such a slow pace. I must find a way to strengthen my resolve. All I can say now is God help me please.

....

Calling Out II

April the 28th. 2006.

Again, I am experiencing another agonizing setback, which I attribute to my lack of dedication and my constant low self-esteem. Now I am very, very fearful of depression, which at this point is growing deeper instead of dissolving. It is just not enough that I realize I cannot overcome this disease alone. I know I need help. What is making it difficult for me is the process necessary to receive the treatment involves courageous kind of effort, meaning the courage to persist in finding, being accepted, and complying with all the preliminary procedures required nowadays to start a program. And having the courage to complete it once the program is started. Nowadays there are waiting lists, especially if you have no medical coverage. The best chance of getting immediate help is having an excellent commercial insurance plan. Even with state insurance medical coverage, it will only give you what I consider second rate treatment options. With no medical insurance, on top of no income, options become limited. This is where my difficulties lie. Government treatment programs for those with no medical coverage and no income do not offer the quality of treatment you could receive if you have name brand commercial insurance. That is why for me, I would need to have the courage and dedication to accept the process that accompanies the low-quality procedures available to me. I cannot fault anyone other than myself for being in this predicament. I know that for me to overcome this disease, I will have to display and maintain a desire that will help me to transcend my desires to have a substance free lifestyle. For me to do so will be a separate struggle. One which I eventually would have to undertake just to get into a program that I will struggle with to complete. And by not receiving the quality type of treatment private rooms program provide It will more likely, be due to my willingness to change that I will succeed in a government sponsored program. I think that for me it will take high quality, very intense, and a very structured treatment, along with my willingness, for me to successfully complete a recovery program. Government sponsored programs are more geared to groups. That is, they are more geared to treatments in groups. This is understandable because this is how they cut down on costs. But at the same time, they are cutting down the quality of care it requires to successfully treat severe substance abuse. In most cases, the treatments for distinct types of addictions vary from addict to addict. Crack addiction cannot always be treated in the same manner as heroin addiction or alcoholic addiction. Most second third-rate programs feel you can put them in the same group and prescribe the same type of treatment program. Even someone with the same addiction to the same drug in some cases needs distinct types of treatment. A person who uses a drug intravenously has a different kind of addiction than one who snorts or one who smokes the same drug. Thus, different methods are needed. This is what a quality treatment program provides. I believe Government programs cannot provide these specialized treatments because of the financial cost. So, unless I can afford my own medical coverage, I will have to accept whatever quality of program that is available.

Ideally, I would prefer a situation where I can enter a quality program immediately with the sufficient method of paying for this type of situation. I know I will receive the highest quality. This would give me the level of comfort and confidence that I would prefer, allowing me to absorb every aspect I need to not only complete the program, but in addition position me to transfer my treatment into a situation where I can help others overcome this disease of addiction. This is my ultimate wish. Because it will allow me to return and share the knowledge I have obtained after the many years of abuse.

Understanding that seeking outside help requires courage, commitment, determination, and willpower.

■■■

Two Days of Being Assaulted by Outside Forces

May 7th, 2006

The last two days have been beyond frustrating, causing me to have undue stress which led to the extremely low period I am currently in. The last two days have been a revelation, which has clearly demonstrated the lengths people will go to obtain their goals, even if it also brings others down. I have been lied to, deceived, picked on and even experienced the pain which happens when a person is treated with less respect and consideration a rabid animal might receive. The first of these two days were filled with words of wisdom. Concern, understanding and respect for facing my demons head on. The very next day, all respect was gone, and in fact, I had to hear the word that made me believe that the first words of encouragement were just words spoken by someone who really had no concern for my well-being. To hear the words "I don't care" after previously hearing what at first, I perceive as an attempt to understand. But I later saw the selfish nature of the entire previous conversation.

On the 5th of May. My former boss asked me if I would work the weekend and my old job, which in late November I left due to the depth. Of my substance abuse, which was starting to get completely out of control. There were other occasions when he asked me to do so, but I refused because deep down I knew once I got back into that environment, my old habit would resurface. And the foundation I was working on to build my willpower would be damaged. But on this occasion, while my first mind was still refusing, I accepted. This decision to accept was due to the so-called encouragement of my mother. Little did I know she had her own interest in my doing so but did not share them at that time. Instead, she chose to point out how eventually I would have to face those things. And I should stop being afraid. I told her fear was what I used to keep alive. But she persists. So, I figured I would go back to give some financial help, knowing it would not be much.

The first day was just as bad as I thought it would be. And then it got worse. Another self-centering individual who had a personal vendetta against me, made up for two of the most stressful days I had had in a while. So now I am fighting my personal demon, my mother's manipulation, and my supervisor's pettiness. Along with rude and idiotic customers- because I worked in a store. All these issues together caused my level of stress to reach critical mass. I was left to face these causes of stress and deal with them alone. And the times when my supervisor could not aggravate me, she would go to another level of pettiness. My mother would also do a complete 360 when I did not give her money, which my supervisor would attempt to deny portions of in her own petty way. Suddenly, Mom does not care about anything else. Which became apparent despite her attempts at denying it. My boss knew I did not want to collaborate with this supervisor. So, he intentionally neglected to mention that the other guy who I thought I would be working with would not be there for a day or two. Had I known this in advance, I never would have gone back no matter what. The strange thing is that my mother insisted on defending my boss's deception. She did not seem to care at all about what I had to deal with. And the only reason I did so was to help her, not myself. This unselfish gesture now has cost me dearly.

Again, I am at the point where I must overcome another setback. It seems like the harder I try to fight, the more intense the attacks become. And now I am starting to feel like I am receiving no support at this crucial moment. It is as if the only way I will overcome this demon's hold on me is to do so with absolutely no support or outside help. My only hope is if God himself intervenes. And he does so despite my lack of effort and willpower. I will not give up. Even an obvious defeat. I will not let my spirit be discouraged, no matter how much I become discouraged. And I will keep hope and continue to believe that one day I will be successful. I know that if I do not, the end will come. One way or another. The end will come.

It is possible that a demon can manifest itself against you through others around you.

■■■

February the 14th, 2007.

It should be quite clear to anyone reading this. That I have been involved in such a battle where my victories have been rare. The dates. Indicate my disappointments and my state of mind. The previous logs in this diary have contained no significant sustained effort to put an end to my hopeless depression, which always goes hand in hand with my substance abuse. It gives me no satisfaction that I will not be able to overcome this uncontrollable abuse. Now I am certain there is no way to overcome this disease without at least two particularly important conditions. Without them, I know I am doomed. First, I must have faith in God. That is necessary. Next, I also must find, develop, and then maintain some level of willpower. This is something I have not had for such a long time. When it comes to resisting, I fail miserably. I guess I could add external support with the other two conditions. In any case, the only thing I can do is ask for God's help in finding a solution to the fundamental problem in willpower.

■■■

Summation

These are diary logs that I kept from 2002 to 2007. You may have noticed the gaps in the dates. This is not all due to lost pages. There were a few that were not included. This is mainly because the few that were not included did not reflect the impact the abuse was having on my life.

The gaps also show my struggle and inconsistent effort to fight the demons. There were periods when I did not have the drive or determination to consistently keep logs.

There were times when I could abstain from using drugs for a brief period, but I was never able to overcome the other demons that accompany addiction. This included anxiety and depression. These were the main feelings Satan used that made it difficult for me to resist the desire to use substances. I needed the drugs just to address those feelings. As I said before, I often failed, miserably and more times than I can recall. Again, these are just my thoughts written down as they happened. Which is why there are gaps in the dates. At the time I was writing these I really thought my family would be reading them after my death. I was surprised when I discovered them in a notebook that I had not opened in about ten years. I am sharing these now to demonstrate how much of a struggle it is to overcome the demon of substance abuse. The only way I can share this is because of faith in my Creator.

When we engage in spiritual war with Satan and his demons- which substance abuse battles are, we need spiritual tools which only our Creator can provide.

Demons can also reflect your actions in others you may meet. In one diary entry I talked about how I felt I was being assaulted and manipulated by my mother, my supervisor, and my boss. Truth is, these were some very decent individuals who I later understood may have made decisions regarding their actions towards me based upon them being temporarily possessed by the demon that was manifesting in me. Particularly my mother who is a Christian through and through. My demons affected her treatment of me at the time.

With all these individuals I mentioned, and many more I did not, I could only hope and pray that any possessions I may have been responsible for in their lives were temporary.

So, there you have it. The journals of a former demon possessed addict. I pray it will encourage someone to never feel like you are standing by the ocean, and it is too big to cross. You will not be able to do it alone and there is the possibility of drowning, ask for help.

Overcoming substance abuse requires a spiritual transformation first. The spirit must be renewed before the body and soul can be successfully renewed. There is always hope and help. Take it from someone who was carried across the ocean of addiction. I cannot say it was on a luxury yacht, but it was not a rowboat. Either way, I made it across.

CHAPTER II

We all know the challenges of living everyday life. And it seems as the older we get the more challenges we face. Challenges are meant to do just that, challenge us. Challenges are beneficial, they help us grow and evolve both mentally and physically.

If we are not challenged to do better, then it becomes less likely we will advance as a society. We have all heard the phrase "life is hard." It is hard and unfair at times, but it is what it is, and we were given the tools to not only survive it but thrive in it.

Challenges shape us one way or another, meaning we can overcome them or allow them to overcome us. Addressing challenges can also be stressful and add pressure. It is important that we learn to accept challenges so we can learn how to cope with them. Being able to cope with them regulates the level of stress and the amount of pressure that everyone will face in life. A person under the influence of addiction feels pressure on another level.

Speaking from personal experience, during my many years as someone addicted to opioids, in particular heroin, every day was filled with pressure (I was an abuser for over twenty-five years). During that time, the stress of maintaining my daily habit put pressure on all areas of my life. The stress would affect my sleeping, eating, parenting, overall health and working. There were other areas but the ones I mentioned are the most important ones. How is this done?

■■■

Day to Day Stress

It does not take long for the demon of addiction to completely take over someone's life.

Once I became dependent on heroin there was no function I could conduct because my body had a craving. Craving any type of substance shuts down the desire for anything else.

In my case I could not do, nor did I desire to do anything until I had satisfied that craving. Whenever I did not have heroin when I awoke, my only thoughts were how and where I would acquire the drug, and not knowing whether I may or may not be able to satisfy the craving was incredibly stressful. Every day it was a challenge and even when I did manage to satisfy my cravings, I knew I had to repeat the process again the next day.

■■

Levels of Stress

The pressure that came with my addiction was generated by the stress I felt due to my worrying. I worried about different problems that could come up that would interrupt my drug use. During that time, I experienced various levels of stress.

■■■

What Do I Mean by Various Levels of Stress?

Whenever I solved the problem of having the money to purchase drugs, that was one level of stress eliminated. Then came the pressure of finding the drug. That is another level of stress eliminated. Then came the pressure not being caught by police officers with drugs on my person, which is another level of stress eliminated. Now imagine after all that someone sold you what we called a "dummy package," which meant the entire process must begin again from the start.

The pressure that comes from the levels of stress I just described is conducted daily. Having a steady source of income may relieve some stress. Having a steady supply may reduce it even more. But the possibility of winding up in jail is never going away if you continue to use drugs. The last level of stress was the one that caused the most damage for me. If I had more money, it would not have been so painful when I bought what I thought was heroin and turned out to be everything but. There was one instance when I was sold instant coffee in place of heroin.

To start the entire process over again with no money and no way to get more is what leads to desperation. It would have been almost impossible for me to go to work or do anything else if I had not satisfied my cravings.

■■■

Mental and Physical Manifestations

The mental effect of drugs will vary from individual to individual. Some maintain some form of décor and others do not value decorum as much or at all. During my time as an addict, I considered myself as somewhere in the middle. Some days I leaned more to the right and sometimes I leaned to the left.

During my time as an addict, my mentality remained intact and honestly to some degree, it increased. If I was not under a great amount of pressure, which was only when I did not have cravings. I was able to continue to grow mentally and spiritually. I was able to tune in to the progressions of the world and understand the impacts of them on our society. At this point, I was not using heroin for pleasure anymore. I was using it to maintain my mental and physical health.

Being under the pressures that I described earlier that accompanied my addiction put an enormous amount of stress on my body physically.

Everyone has heard the saying, "pressure bursts pipes." Pressure of any kind affects our physical health in several ways, some of which are deadly.

Loss of appetite, and poor hygiene are quite common among addicts. Both necessities revolved around my drug use. It was difficult for me to practice good hygiene and I could not eat and enjoy a meal without using it first. And the strange thing for me was that eating reduced the effect the drug had on me, so I would have to use more after I had eaten. There were days when I could not eat or drink because those were the days when I had no drugs. It was during these periods when I was starving my body for the nutrients it needed to maintain my physical health. Depriving the body of the necessary nutrients puts a lot of stress on our organs which will cause them not to function as they should. I have had friends who were diagnosed with a condition due to organ malfunction but had no idea it was occurring because of their substance abuse. And I know some who have died from a condition they were not even aware was affecting them. Though I have never used one, those who use needles to inject drugs into their systems increase their risks of infections and veins being obstructed, ruptured, or collapsed.

Pain is a mechanism that informs the body when something is wrong, in most instances. Opioids are pain suppressors, so if someone is a regular user, their body is less likely to register pain if there is a problem. Also, anyone with a pre-existing condition like asthma, hyper-tension, diabetes, etc. can experience rapid deterioration of their condition and not be aware of it.

The stress caused by the thought of diseases and organ failure due to my abuse, and watching and hearing how others were stricken and died not knowing they were ill, and the fear these incidents generated, was the primary reason I began to look for a way out of my opioid addiction.

During my addiction, the mental stress and the physical stress manifested themselves equally. The pressure was mounting for me to do something about it before it was too late.

Other aspects of my life were affected by my substance abuse. I was fired from many jobs because of my addiction.

In relationships, my one marriage was strained and ended due to my substance abuse. After that I had many romantic relationships but could not commit because I was already committed to heroin. And some were nice respectable women (the one-nighters were with other addicts).

There was a strain on the relationship with my mother who had to witness a lot of my abusive activities because most of that time I lived in her house. All my siblings were aware of my abuse but were never judgmental. In a later chapter I will share how my sisters, sister-in-law, and my brother helped me through my last days of being an addict, though I did face criticism from them.

Parenting and grand parenting is the one aspect that at the time, I agonized over the most. Here is where I felt inadequate.

Regarding my children, I did everything I could to cover up my addiction when they were with me. The older they got, the harder this would become. I was afraid that I would not be around to watch them become the successful, productive citizens and parents that they all turned out to be, despite little input from me. Same with the grandchildren when they were born. The fear of dying and not watching them grow up as I have, had also given me a reason to change my way of life. Pressure like this I did not see coming.

There is enough everyday pressure that we must face during a lifetime. Being an addict brings additional pressure and on so many levels.

It is a biological fact that prolonged stress will shorten a person's life. Someone may choose to use drugs, but they do not choose to become an addict. Addiction was the side effect of my substance abuse.

Because of the initial pleasure, there is little that can be done to deter someone from using drugs. This is something that can be witnessed by observing the opioid crisis currently happening in this country.

People are dying from the drug fentanyl while others are looking to purchase drugs that could be laced with this deadly product.

The demon of addiction affects the mind and body of the user. The fear of dying or becoming disabled is lessened by the power the demon has over a person through addiction. The stress, the pressure and the fear of failure can all be overcome through prayer and meditation. I cannot stress enough just how much these "tools" helped me overcome my demons. In the next chapter I am going to share what I was pressured to do to save my life.

CHAPTER III

Written in the book of James, in chapter 2 the Bible teaches us about "Faith and Deeds". Starting at vs 17 it states that, "faith by itself, if not accompanied by action is dead". And in vs 18 the second sentence reads, "Show me your faith without deeds, and I will show you my faith by my deeds". What is James trying to say? To explain this, I am going to use myself as an example.

For over thirty-five years I used several types of drugs. Starting in 1975 I was introduced to heroin. And by 1986 it became my primary drug of choice. Though I continued to indulge occasionally in other forms of abuse, (cocaine, PCP, LSD, and of course pot and alcohol), heroin was always included. During that period, I held a steady job and started a family until my company folded in 1988. From that time until I entered a treatment center, I was living off charity. Let me explain.

After the separation from my wife in 1985, (for obvious reasons), I began to exclude the other substances I was using. Crack cocaine was becoming popular at that time and of course I became a regular user. This was a real dilemma because the crack required me to spend more money on it than I was spending on heroin, which I had to have if I was doing crack. So, when the company I was working for closed in 88, I had to rely on my unemployment payments which were only about two thirds of my working salary. After the separation from my wife, I went to live with my mother and when unemployment ran out around the end of 88, I needed to find a job. That summer is when I started living off charity.

The Proceeds Went to Drugs: I started and was fired from four jobs between the fall of 1988 until the winter of 1991. Each dismissal was due to my addiction. I was not making enough money to support my addiction and I could not work unless I had heroin in my pocket when it was time to punch in.

All four of those employment opportunities amounted to charitable contributions to my substance abuse. From 1992 until 2011 I was living off charity. The longest I was ever able to hold a job during that time was eighteen months before I was fired and then rehired, on many occasions, sometimes after only three or four months and all at the same Food and Liquor store. And the money I was paid was no more than charitable contributions to my substance abuse.

The times when I had no job were the times when I suffered the most. I would do anything to get money for drugs. I even sold drugs for someone else briefly, -of course, this was a bad idea. Odd jobs from family members or friends were like heaven sent, but they were few. It was during this period (1998) when my desire to continue down this road began to change. I started to tell myself that unless something happens to change my life, I was going to die an addict. I was waiting for something to happen that would change my life. But I was not doing anything to make it happen.

■■

Healing for a Lame Beggar (*or an addict*)

Acts Chapter 3:1 (KJV)

*One day, Peter and John were going up to the temple at the time of prayer at 3:00 in the afternoon. **Verse 2** Now a man who was lame from birth was being carried to the temple gate called Beautiful., where he was put every day to beg from those going into the temple courts. **Verse 3**. When he saw Peter and John about to enter, he asked them for money. **Verse 4**. Peter looked straight at him, as did John. Then Peter said, "**look at us.**" Verse five. So, the man gave them his attention, expecting to get something from them. **Verse six.** Then Peter said, "**Silver or gold I do not have, but what I do have, I give you. in the name of Jesus Christ of Nazareth walk.**" Taking him by the right hand, he helped him up and instantly the man's feet and ankles became strong. **Verse 8.** He jumped to his feet and began to walk.*

The beggar referred to in these scriptures had been lame for forty years and as so, he was unable to make it to the temple for daily prayer without others carrying him. Once there he could beg the crowds for money. He was counting on their charity to provide enough money for him to get through the day just so he could repeat the process on the next day. This is what my life was like for about twenty years. I was like the lame beggar. The four jobs I was fired from, the multiple firings from another one, plus odd jobs here and there, were only charitable contributions to get me through my addiction for a day so I could do it all over again the next day.

Starting around 2002, I was beginning to lose hope in ever overcoming my addiction. It was difficult to maintain and the pressure to do so generated a huge amount of stress. Because of this, I began to seriously ask God for help. I had prayed before for something to happen that would change my life but now, I am starting to feel hopeless and desperate.

■■

"Look At Us"

This quote from Peter is from **Acts 3 verse 4**, where he says this to the beggar to get his **attention.**

Once I started praying to God to do something to change my path, I was looking to receive a form of charity. I thought that because I had finally seen where my life was heading, God would ease my journey. The truth is He had reached out to do so on many occasions, but I had ignored Him. I had never realized this until years later when I began to reflect on my journey. He was trying to get my **attention** before the time would come when I would be asking Him for "silver and gold" or charity. It was not until God saw that he had my attention that my prayers to Him would begin to be answered, and I could be given the opportunity to "walk" on my own like the lame beggar or in my case to stop counting on the drug which only positioned me to seek charitable contributions from others for my survival. If I was going to survive this addiction, I needed to be able to take the necessary steps to initiate the process on my own.

Not only did the lame beggar gain the ability to walk, but he also now did not have to beg for a living. He could now work and earn a living as every able person should do. And in **verse 6** of the scripture, we see that by invoking the name "Jesus Christ of Nazarene", the power of the Holy Spirit flowed through Peter allowing him to take the beggar by the hand and raise him up. - Lazarus was raised by the power that flowed through Jesus, not by Him. But Peter had to get his attention first and though the lame beggar was looking for charity from Peter, he ended up with something of greater use.

I shared this story because it is a near description of how our Creator delivered me from addiction. It was not until I became desperate that I began to "Look" for His healing instead of His charity.

My lameness was due to my drug abuse which I turned into a disability. I became unable to "walk / work" without the drugs carrying me. The times I did manage to "walk / work," it was only to get more drugs to get me through that day. Living this way of life is highly stressful. Having this type of disability meant I would never be able to live the quality, productive, fulfilling, joyful life that I now wanted. I thought I would forever be a lame charity case.

Once I finally stopped looking for charity, I was shown that I could have the fulfilling life I wanted. What I needed was God's healing, not His charity. He was not going to just give me the easy path to becoming drug free that I would have preferred. That would have amounted to charity.

I think that because I had not given Him my attention previously, now I was going to have to get up and "walk / work" for my healing, which I inevitably did. The healing I received came through the Holy Spirit, which I have already shared in this and the previous book: **The Effective use of Spiritual Tools.**

The message here is that some of us ask God through our prayers for help. We ask for his continued grace and mercies which He gives freely. But those of us who have in the past rejected, ignored, or disobeyed Him may be required to show a different measure of faith before He answers our prayers. I spent years asking Him for trivial things that I thought would ease the pains of addiction instead of asking for healing. The healing I received was awarded to me and the joy of being drug free is more than I asked for. Being restored after being disabled for decades is better than "silver and gold."

CHAPTER IV

There is a saying that " you don't realize what you had until it's gone". And as we know it means we do not value the things we should until they are taken from us, or we lose them. In this chapter I am going to share some of the many things that were taken from me because of substance abuse.

As the oldest in my family, I was expected to look after my younger siblings. At first it was an irritating burden because it required me to sacrifice some of my play time. But as time went by, I learned to be protective of them. It is something that I still do. This development gave me the ability to have compassion not only for my family but also for people overall. With compassion comes the desire to help others, especially those in need. But to do so you must have the capacity and the assets.

What substance abuse did at the time was allow Satan to steal my capabilities and my assets. I still maintained my compassion, but my ability to commit acts of charity was stolen, along with some other things.

■■

How did Satan do this?

It happened because the unnatural spirit of substance abuse was controlling me. It took me out of position to protect my assets and Satan was able to come in and steal them from me. Satan uses substance abuse to incapacitate or at least weaken the abuser so there is no resistance when he comes to steal. Some are not aware or do not care when their assets are stolen. I was disappointed because, not only did I allow him to come in and steal my assets, but he also stole my resources. I did not have the capacity anymore to protect them.

We are required to have the capacity to be resourceful, which is how we gain our assets. Because I had all these stolen from me, my spirit, -which was the only thing I had left, was extremely low and Satan was coming for that next.

In my case it was the sin of substance abuse and the subsequent sins I committed because of the abuse, which took me out of position and allowed Satan and many of his helpers to come in and rip me off.

■■■

How Did I Recover What Was Stolen?

Because my spirit was extremely low, I had no choice but to seek help from our Creator. I guess it can be said that I reported the thefts to Him. I prayed to the source of all there is for help, and from that instant on things began to improve.

I had prayed many times before, but I had not reached the point where I would recognize His hand at work when my prayers were answered. When I did recognize it, He revealed to me what I needed to do. Praying was the first step. And the next step to recovering that which had been stolen was getting treatment for the addiction. It took a painstaking and patient testing effort for me to find and enter a treatment facility. Once there I was determined to do whatever it took and stay as long as necessary to complete this step towards recovering what was stolen.

Since completing a substance abuse program, - which I was guided to by His hand, I have regained the capacity to find the resources I needed to build up the assets I wanted to use to help others. This book along with my You Tube videos are some of the assets I use to help those who are looking for help. For me it is like sowing a seed. I will share more about my seed sowing later.

CHAPTER V

The last time I used heroin was on February 27th, 2011. On the morning of the 28th I was checking into a 90-day treatment program. To describe my eagerness to start my recovery is like describing a NASA Space Shuttle launch.

I am a huge aeronautics fan and I get a huge thrill from watching rocket launches. Before each launch, the rocket or as I mentioned, shuttle-which is attached to many rockets, is slowly moved from its hangar to the launching pad.

Through the 27th of February I was living with my mother in her basement, or my "hanger". On that day I spent most of my time preparing myself physically for the 28th, the day I was to start treatment. I had been mentally prepared for days and now I was doing what I needed to do to remove the material items that were a part of my substance abuse.

My launch time was 6am from a location on the other side of town so I needed transportation for me and my personal belongings –which was not much. After three and a half weeks my launch date was finally upon me. On the eve of the 27th, my son would transport me from my mother's house to my daughter's apartment because of her proximity to the hospital where I was to be picked up and transported to the treatment facility (like the shuttle being transported from its hanger to the launching pad). To further describe how eager I was to begin my treatment, think of a fighter jet launching from the deck of an aircraft carrier. The last thing the pilot does after being cleared for take-off is salute the deck hand as a gesture of thanks for guiding him safely into launch position. When my daughter pulled up to the hospital, I jumped out of the car and was heading for the entrance then I heard her say "hey, wait a minute, I didn't even get a hug." I was so eager to launch that I did not give her that thank you and a so long hug, or "salute."

■■■

Launching Into the Unknown Present's Challenges

There were a few challenges I had to face just to get into a program. The entire process produced obstacles which I believe were by design. They were put there to challenge my sincerity, dedication, and commitment to doing what was necessary for me to put my addiction behind me forever. None of this came easy for me.

■■■

Obstacle One: The Intake Process

My first challenge in the quest for recovery was finding a treatment facility. It takes a desire to change the way one is living to take this step. Next comes making and keeping the appointment. This is where things became challenging for me. I was given a date that was five days after I first contacted the intake coordinator. For me this meant I had to figure out a way to supply my habit for five days with no money to do so. There were some horrible periods of withdrawals that were so bad I was forced to beg for money. Had it not been for my half-brother sending me some help I do not believe I would have made my appointment.

The intake process is a necessary one that is required to enter any treatment program. The procedures differ from program to program, depending upon the way one is treated. For instance, the process for out-patient treatment is different for those who seek in-patient treatment. The results rely on timing and access, especially for in-patient programs because space must be available to accommodate someone for the duration of the stay. The process for me was more than challenging.

As I was heading to the intake office for my first prescreening, I was very hopeful that this horrible life I was living was about to change. And I believed it would change in a day or two. After the pre-screening, I was told something that turned my hope into horror. I was told that it would be three weeks before they had a bed for me. For an addict with no income, three weeks seems like forever. How was I going to survive until the end of the month? Detours like these were divinely placed for a purpose. But because of the veil of addiction, I was unable to see the hand of the almighty working for me. It was only in hindsight that I came to recognize this.

■■

Obstacle Two: Red Tape

I cannot overlook my half-brother's help at that time. It was him that suggested the treatment program I would attend, and as I stated he initially made contributions that carried me, but toward the end of the waiting period his assistance was even more timely.

At that time in my life, I had no type of identification credentials. During the intake interview I was told I would need a state issued ID or something with my name and address on it from the state of Illinois or the city of Chicago. I had nothing. I called back a couple of days later and asked if there was any other type of ID card they would accept, and I was told I could use a Photo ID issued for free by a place that found temporary housing for the homeless. This was fantastic news for two reasons, one it was free, and two, the office was near to my home, one problem, I had no money which meant I had no way of getting there. I called my half-brother who lived miles away from me and told him the situation and by the grace of God he happened to be just around the corner visiting an aunt. He took me to get the ID I needed, and it was on to the next obstacle.

■■

Obstacle Three: Family Notification

By now most of my family was aware of my addiction. For years some of them have tried to counsel me in one way or another. The fact is that they truly did not understand my struggle. Their view was that it was something I enjoyed doing and that I was not aware of the control the drug had over my life. Part of this misperception came from my personality which was being a levelheaded individual before I started using drugs and, during my addiction.

Now they have been made aware, by me and my half-brother, that I have been accepted into a treatment program. This is when I noticed the presence of a divine spirit.

As I mentioned, it was going to take about three weeks before my treatment began. And as I said, I had no money and no job to support my habit until then. I can think of no other time during my addiction where a family member would knowingly give me money, making it possible for me to buy drugs. A few of them did unknowingly, or they may not have been sure, but if anyone were sure they would never make that kind of contribution. This was about to change, but why now?

In hindsight, a spirit came over them, not all but especially two of my sisters and my sister-in-law. They saw the sincerity in my efforts to transform my life and being Christians, they felt a responsibility to do their part to help see me through the lengthy period of waiting for the date I am to start treatment to arrive. They knowingly, - at that time and no other before, - helped me get what I needed to get me through to that launch date, which in turn gave me the determination to complete the process that I had started at all costs. There were some other family members who made contributions, and there were some who refused to do so based on their principles, but these three did so without hesitation. To say the least, it made my waiting period pass smoother than I expected.

I was able to overcome these obstacles with the aid of an unseen force. But the challenges were not over yet.

■■■

Into the Unknown

Earlier I mentioned how eager I was to begin treatment for substance abuse. I had a plan in place going into the process. There is a choice of a 30, 60, or a 90-day program. I chose the 90-day program, and I broke my approach down into 30-day increments. For the first 30 days I would sit back and absorb. The next 30 days I would reveal what I already knew about treatment and determine if what was being done in counseling sessions would apply to me. And the last 30 days was to be geared towards preparations for my reentry into society. It was the plan I executed but not without challenges.

After being pre-screened at the hospital on the 28th of February and given a dose of methadone, (I was entering a medicated treatment program and methadone is given to opioid abusers to ease the withdrawal symptoms), I had to wait over five hours for a bus to come pick me and a couple of others up to transport us to the treatment facility located in a small town outside the city.

After about a 90-minute drive we arrive and do our onsite screening process where we are asked questions about the level of our addiction. This gives them an idea of how to medically treat the addiction. Because I had cut down on my consumption before I got there, - mainly because I could only afford a small amount at a time, I was prescribed an exceptionally low daily dosage of methadone and was told they would gradually reduce the dosage, and I would be done in two weeks. I told the nurse I will be done in one week.

Afterwards I was assigned a room and was told that after dinner I did not have to attend meetings. This is their practice with everyone on their first day. I attended anyway.

The next morning, I went back to the city to see a general practitioner to assess my overall health. I was told my blood pressure needed to be lowered and I would have to return in another week. Now I am taking methadone and blood pressure meds daily.

My first few days were spent adjusting to life in a controlled environment. Rules were explained and I was assigned to a counselor who expressed her expectations and listened to mine.

On the next appointment day, I am feeling very sluggish, and I am not sure why. So, I am grouchy and complaining because this trip is unnecessary. It is a 2-hour round trip and after seeing the doctor we must wait until the van comes back to pick us up. While we are seeing doctors – usually there is a small group going at the same time, the driver is either picking up new clients from the city or waiting at another hospital for another patient. This time was the longest wait of the three, (There is a final doctor's visit required before being released from the program).

After I saw the doctor, I waited almost four hours before I was picked up. I was very aggravated by now and just wanted this day to be over with. Every time we go out and return, we must give a urine sample to be tested. This tells them if someone used drugs while they were out (some were allowed out to take care of personal matters, but we all had to drop). This was also irritating because I could not go to my room until I gave my urine sample.

■■■

Now I Get It

The first thing we do every morning after breakfast is stand in the med-line. It is where we are issued our daily doses of whatever medications required. As I said in my case it was blood pressure medication and methadone. When I got to the nurse for my daily dosage, she only gave me the pressure pills and told me I was done with the" methadone maintenance" portions. They had been weening me off my low dose methadone from the second day I got here. The day she told me this was exactly one week after I got there, just as I had said. It explained why I was so sluggish and cranky the day before. Each day afterwards I began to feel better. My plan was coming along but there were more challenges to come.

Note: for all those years I was using drugs, I had wondered about my health. I had seen friends die from underlying conditions they were not aware of because of their substance abuse. It had always been my fear that I was suffering from something and was not aware of it.

When I visited the doctor that last time, he told me after his examination that everything was fine, heart, lungs, etc. At the time he was telling me that, I was still feeling that sluggishness that I mentioned earlier and after the visit, the long wait was the only thing on my mind. It was not until the next day after learning I no longer had to be given the methadone to ease my withdrawals that I realized that I had been given the answers to questions I had concerning my overall health.

The veil was slowly being removed and I began to see the hand of the Creator operating in this process. From here on there was no turning back, or so I thought.

■■■

Close Call

Now I am about two weeks into the program and as I mentioned earlier, the first 30 days were for me to observe and absorb. The daily meetings are beginning to become monotonous, and I am just waiting for the evening sessions where we usually have a guest speaker. It is about this time when we are given so-called daily jobs. The jobs ranged from mopping floors to overseeing the entire unit. Mopping floors is like starting from the bottom. This is done to provide structure. I was not a fan of this because all I was there for was to become drug free. This structure had no value for me. Later I would come to embrace the opportunity this idea provided, but that is for later.

It has been a week since I was taken off the methadone, which while I was taking it helped me sleep. Now I am having trouble falling asleep and when I do it may be for only 3 or 4 hours before it is time for me to get up.

Rooms were shared and most had three occupants. I shared a room with two other guys. Also, the rooms were close to one another. And the walls were very thin, which led me to this next challenge.

In this program there are people of all ages, including teenagers. Across from the room I shared there were a group of men who shared a room with a teenager who had been there a little longer than me. During our free time music was allowed if it was not too loud.

As I said I was struggling to fall asleep at night and it made it difficult for me to stay awake in the morning meetings. Things got worse when the young man decided to play his music all night. And it was not just because of the thin walls that I could hear the music, he played it loud. This went on for about two days before I went to him and asked politely if he could turn his music down. Though he said he would, for some reason I knew he would not, and I was right. So, I went to a counselor and reported my problem. Now others were disturbed by the loud music but no one else said anything. It was because of this, and she liked the kid that the counselor did nothing about the music, even though there were rules against playing loud music during any part of the day. I was at a crossroad. My recovery process is in jeopardy and the people in charge do not seem to be willing to do anything about it. I must do something.

After another night of not sleeping due to the loud music, I decided to leave. I had prayed for a decision to be made by God because I was there by His will, and I was struggling for a resolution. I could not get any sleep which made it difficult to pay attention in daily meetings. These conditions were interfering with my recovery. My solution, I am going to call my daughter in the morning and have her drive all the way out here and pick me up.

That night I slept in my jacket and hat, had all my things packed up and was just waiting for morning to call my daughter. I listened to Celo Green all night long singing "forget you" (I cannot write what I was thinking at the time). The next morning a different counselor came looking for the young man because he had not shown up for his daily job of running the kitchen for breakfast. When she entered his room to wake him up, she did something that reminded me that God was in control. My solution was not going to be THE solution. She took the radio and told him he would not get it back until his discharge date.

I could not believe what had just happened. I immediately came out of my room and told her she was my hero (she may have been wondering why I had a hat and jacket on, but she never inquired). Again, a Divine Spirit had stepped in on my behalf. There is no other explanation.

 The remainder of the first thirty days passed without further incidents.

...

Time To Leave the Reservation

During this thirty-day period is when I began to be more expressive during daily meetings. I began to share more of my knowledge of not just being an addict, but concerning life in general, especially spiritually.

I spent the last ten or so years of my addiction, looking for spiritual help. I would watch a Christian TV channel for programs by different pastors, evangelists, and prophets looking for inspiration and encouragement. The program that helped me the most were the ones broadcasted by the pastor of a church in Fayetteville Arkansas. The name of the program was called the Shepards Chappel by Pastor A.

Murray. In his program he taught from the Bible, "chapter by chapter and verse by verse."

I was able to watch them often because his shows aired back-to-back starting at about 3am until 6am during the week and because I was still using drugs at this hour, I would be awake most nights. My fascination developed with this "Man of God" because he had an uncanny way of answering a specific question I may have asked before I saw his program. During the time I was seeking answers, he was answering my questions and addressing many specific concerns I had then. His teachings helped me get a better understanding about life. His teachings also gave me a better understanding of how demons operate. Even though I was an addict, I was growing in spirituality. I just did not know it at the time.

Daily meetings were conducted by various counselors using distinctive styles as one would expect. The spirituality aspect was mildly introduced and mildly discussed as a starting point for recovery. In the classes I attended, the counselors quickly saw that I could connect their secular teachings to a spiritual source. What I recognized was that a lot of what they were trying to convey could be traced to the teachings found in the Bible. I took on the task of simplifying the lessons so anyone who did not understand them, (helping others understand would be something the staff would require me to do later). I was off the "sit quietly for now reservation" and there was no turning back. Unfortunately for me there was a challenge waiting because I allowed this assertiveness to go to my head.

■■■

A Humbling Experience

I mentioned earlier that everyone was given "jobs" or daily responsibilities. There were custodians, cafeteria workers, communication, laundry, and kitchen workers. The high-level spots were the Department Heads. These individuals oversaw the functions of each department and reported to the Head of Communications, who oversaw the entire unit. Those who worked in communications were responsible for assisting the regular communication staff during the week. And on weekends when the staff were off the department was run solely by the clients.

In the middle of my second thirty-day period I was given the Head of Communications position. Each position is discussed and issued by the facility staff and counselors. Overseeing the entire unit gave me a different sense of responsibility compared to clarifying the lessons and discussions during daily meetings. I was being challenged to be a leader which was new to me. But I was about to be taught a lesson in humility.

As the leader it was my responsibility alone to make sure things ran perfectly. This thought alone is one I would come to regret.

As the leader, I made the work schedule for those working at the communication desk. I had an easy job where all I was supposed to do was hand out assigned shifts, train new people and stop for the day. The words "I was supposed to do" is where the words "I did" should have been. I ended up doing more than I should have, and this formed some resentment by those I was charged with leading.

The mistake I made was not allowing those who were there to perform a task to do so. I took the firsthand, micromanagement approach. When I should have been doing less, I was doing more, or as the saying goes, "doing too much." I did not realize that I should have been letting others do more than me. These positions were designed to help give a sense of responsibility and commitment to those who never had to or were never expected to exhibit when they were using drugs.

I was a very senior client in terms of age (52), and all those I oversaw were young. I did not notice their eagerness to do something that meant more to them than it did to me. I was focusing on my role and not on an opportunity for them. As their leader I should have been focused on helping them develop a sense of commitment and responsibility that some of them may have needed, (the lesson I learned from this experience would turn out to be helpful). Answering the phones and doing customer service was something most of them had never done, and if I were there doing it, someone else who had not had that type of experience could not. I had worked in an office before so this should have been more of an opportunity for them.

The facility staff issued responsibilities bi-weekly. A client could be elevated to another position or re-assigned to another area. For instance, someone could work in the kitchen for one two-week period and move to communications for the next two weeks. The only exceptions are if someone is not performing as required or if for several reasons, they suddenly must leave the program. There are some who remain in their positions until they are discharged but this is up to the staff.

The resentfulness created among those I was supposed to be leading as Head of Communications led those who felt they were not getting an opportunity to take their grievances to the staff, and I was moved to head of the kitchen. It was like a demotion for me, and it left me feeling a bit depressed, which was unexpected. I did not end up with the kitchen position because I was so depressed that I became ill and was unable to function, so the job was given to someone else.

It was during this time of sorrow when something extraordinary occurred. While I was wallowing in my sorrow and feeling disgraced, something happened that snapped me out of my depression.

There is a copy of an affirmation everyone receives when entering the program. It reminds us to keep pushing and to not give in to distractions. I had long ago misplaced my copy, so I had not read it in a while.

As I mentioned, rooms were of multiple occupancy, and some were only separated by the bathroom that had to be shared by both rooms. Since my "demotion," I had been closed off and withdrawn. Only leaving my room to eat if then. I did not even attend meetings and the only reason I got away with this is because the staff thought I was ill (I even convinced the on-site doctor that I was sick). This went on for about two days.

It was on the third day that as I was lying in bed in the late afternoon, I heard one of my neighbors reading the affirmation. Though we were not in the same room I could hear him clearly. He was trying to learn it so he would know it by heart. After hearing the part about not giving in and not being defeated, along with his determination to learn the entire copy, something came over me instantly. I immediately got out of bed and the words I spoke aloud were, "he is absolutely right." I did not come here to be defeated in any way. That moment resurrected my spirit and restored the drive and determination that had fizzled out. I do not recall telling my neighbor what he did for me, but I did thank him. At once I had overcome another challenge but unbeknownst to me, there was a plan in place that would put me on a path that would bring me more gratification than I could have ever imagined. I have just completed day sixty.

■■■

Exit Strategy

For the first week of treatment patients must attend what is known as the "Puddle." Though it was never clearly explained why, I had my own theory of why this meeting was called the "Puddle." I reasoned that a primordial puddle is where life began so this is where a new life will begin for me.

It was where we were given the rules of the program and we had to be able to recall them when asked by our counselor. It was usually led by two patients who had little time left in treatment.

After my semi melt down, I was given the head of the puddle position. At first, I was reluctant to do the job, in fact, I did not show up for the first meeting after being named to the position. When I finally attended, something unexpected happened. I realized that I was given an opportunity to teach. I discovered that I could help guide the newcomers through the start of their treatment process in a way that I was not. And to my surprise, I loved doing it. I did this for the last thirty days of my treatment and what I found was that this was helping me prepare for life after treatment. For the remainder of my daily meetings, I focused on learning more about addiction and how to reach others who suffer from abuse.

The connections I made with those who attended my puddle meetings lasted until it was time for me to leave the program. Many of them came to me for guidance instead of their counselors. Had it not been for that teaching opportunity and the feedback from those I was able to teach, I might not have the passion I have for teaching, and I am sure I would not be writing my second book to date.

■■■

Why I Shared This Experience

Anything we achieve in life will be done with various degrees of effort. Getting good grades in school, buying a house or car, and maintaining good health require different degrees of effort.

Facing and overcoming a deadly situation requires the greatest amount of effort we humans can give. Life threatening circumstances cannot be addressed lightly. Being addicted to a life-threatening drug requires a huge effort to overcome it. Most who struggle with addiction are not able to meet the requirements to overcome their addiction. Addiction is a demonic possession, and no demon is going to allow anyone they possess to have the power to resist them. This is why it is extremely hard for an abuser to have the will to get help.

After years of being controlled by the demon of addiction, I started praying for a way to break free and I began to develop the will to resist the influence of the demon that had possessed me for so long. It all started with prayer.

Part of resisting required me to reject what I had become. Along with this came dissatisfaction, disgust, and finally desperation. I wanted a better and more importantly a healthier life than the one I had been living and I had to be the one to do something to bring about a change.

What I discovered was all I needed to do was have the courage and desire to take the first step, and out of that desperation came first the desire, then the courage. Once I took that initial step, things started to fall into place. Seeing this happen let me know that a force was working in my favor. A force that had been waiting on me to activate it in my favor. And as I said, it all began with prayer.

Getting into that 90-day treatment program took efforts I never thought I had within me. I know who the source of that force was that guided me throughout my time in treatment. Throughout that entire time there was one challenge after another. Even in that last week I was penalized for something I had absolutely no control over, but because the offenders were my students, I was punished. Still, it was the best decision I could have made considering the way our God carried me through.

I encourage everyone who is struggling with substance abuse or abuse of any kind to take a moment and pray for help. Make prayer the very first step and if you are willing to listen and obey, your prayers will be answered.

James 1:5 (NIV). *If any of you lacks wisdom, you should ask God, who gives generously to all without finding fault, and it will be given to you.*

CHAPTER VI

All Christians are familiar with the phrase, "if you have a need, sow a seed".

I am not comfortable with sowing seeds to fill a personal need. I must find someone or somewhere that has a need. A seed should be planted so the results can benefit more people than just the planter.

If you are not in position; meaning having the capacity to protect your assets which can be used to help others, then Satan will rip you off. This is why I shared this. In other words, hold your position.

May I encourage you to pick up my book called, The Effective use of Spiritual Tools which shares some of the spiritual tools I used to overcome my demons that ripped me off.

■■

Know Where to Sow

We are all aware of where fruits come from, and the process involved in producing them. There is a starting point for every living organ on this planet and beyond. The universe itself is alive though not in the way we are accustomed to witnessing. The planet itself is alive, it must be to produce life. But from where did it all originate? What is the initial source of everything that is?

The process is started with a seed. In the case of the universe, our Creator used His word as a seed. Even for those who do not believe in a supreme being as the source, whatever they are led to believe that started all of this would be considered the source, or the seed which everything came from. Someone or something started this entire process.

■■■

How Does Seeds Work?

Seeds are genetically designed to produce after its own kind.

In Genesis chapter one there is a law of God that is stated at least 10 times that; everything God has created will produce after its own kind. Everything produces, increases, and multiplies after its own kind. If you plant rice, you are going to get rice. Human seed cannot reproduce plants.

The scientific world has only recently discovered several breakthroughs in DNA transfer. (This transfer assists scientists in cloning). It is amazing to note that God has already ordered this system of transferring the characteristics and traits from one seed to another from the very beginning of creation.

In Matthew chapter 13 Jesus talks about a farmer who went out to plant (sow) his seeds. In verse four he talks about how some of the farmers' seeds had fallen along the path, and birds ate them up. (In Luke's version chapter 8 vs. 5 the seeds were trampled on as well). And in verse five he talks about some of the seeds that had fallen on rocky places where there was not much soil, so they sprang up quickly. In verse six he talked about how when the sun came up, those plants were scorched and withered because they had no root. In verse seven, he talks about how other seeds fell among thorns which grew up and choked the plants. And in verse 8. He talks about how other seeds fell on good soil where they produced a crop. And in verse nine he says, *"he who has ears, let him hear."* This parable sums up the reason it is important that we know where to sow. We want to plant in good soil, to have good crops, so those who desire them will have them. Like the "seed" God planted in the womb of a virgin so that the world could bear witness to the "good news."

∎∎

Chapter VII: Who Should Benefit?

In John chapter 15 vs 5 (NIV) Jesus says, *"I am the vine; you are the branches. If you remain in me, and I in you, you will bear much fruit; apart from me, you can do nothing."*

I mentioned earlier that a seed will produce its own kind. This is the same approach that should be taken when we set out to plant seeds.

Romans 12 vs 6-8 (NIV), *"we have different gifts, according to the grace given to each of us. If your gift is prophesying, then prophesy in accordance with your faith. 7. If it is serving, then serve. If it is teaching, then teach. 8. If it is to encourage, then give encouragement. If it is giving, then give generously. If it is to lead, do it diligently. If it is to show mercy, do it cheerfully.*

If someone is a barber or hair stylist and decides to make a video. It should be about being a barber or hair stylist. The video is a product which can be used to introduce their craft to anyone who desires to learn how to become barbers and stylists. And at the same time, make other stylists and barbers better by sharing tips and information. The video can be a seed and the tips and information can be called fruit.

I am a former substance abuser, specifically opioids. It is because of this; I try to produce content or plant seeds so anyone who has a desire to, can have access to a potential source which could help overcome the demon of addiction. They can do so by accessing my "content tree." It is my responsibility to plant seeds, nurture them until they blossom, and then take care of them to ensure that they produce good fruits. What I am referring to is the videos and books I produce about overcoming substance abuse. They are the seeds I plant and nurture.

In the parables I referenced earlier, Jesus described the results of someone planting seeds in four types of soil: the hard path, a rocky, a thorny, and in good soil. Other than the hard path, every soil could produce a plant of some sort. Planting seeds in the appropriate soil determines the quality of your crops. Each of the four types of soil mentioned represents a way of life. They can also represent a character trait. It is also quite possible that one person can demonstrate all four over their lifetime.

■■

What Does Soil Represent?

On our planet soil represents many things in life. Soil is where we plant not only organic items, but non-organics as well, such as ideas. Soil can be a place where our hopes and dreams grow. But just as with everything else in life there is good soil and bad soil.

Demonic seeds can also be planted in bad soil. Our spirits, our souls, and our hearts can be considered soil. Our personalities are shaped according to those three areas. If a demon is allowed to plant a seed in either one of those areas the soil will become contaminated. This is how and where addiction begins. Once any one of these areas become compromised the mind and body will follow.

Soil is also represented in our education, science, and technological institutions. Seeds planted in these areas do have an impact on society. But again, it is important that we plant the right seeds.

Christians along with recovering addicts, ex-convicts, or anyone who has overcome the worst situations our society has to offer, are "high value targets" for Satan.

His number one priority is to have those who worship our Creator and our redeemer to stop doing so and worship him. His next task is to keep those who do not know Jesus or have strayed away from Him, from knowing that we have rulership over him. Satan wants to have humankind serve him though humanity was not meant to do so.

Satan has his own seeds, but he needs our soil to plant them in. He cannot plant his bad seeds in good soil. Good soil will reject Satan's bad seeds. When we choose to accept the Holy Spirit into our lives, our hearts and minds will become good soil. All good soil is tended to by believers in Christ and protected by the Holy Spirit.

It will be up to those who preach, teach, and evangelize to plant good seeds as well as tend to the growth of the product. One can only plant a good seed if they themselves are the product of a good seed planted in good soil. And it is possible to be uprooted and replanted as I consider myself to have been. Any addict, criminal, etc. can be uprooted and replanted in "good soil." After I was replanted, it took some time for me to absorb the "spiritual nutrients" that "good soil" provides. Over time I began to describe myself not as being replanted but as someone who has been transplanted from soil that was not lifegiving to a brand-new garden. I believe this to be true but another way to prove it is by planting my own seeds and waiting for the results. I hope anyone reading this is benefiting from my "fruit tree."

CHAPTER VIII

This guy falls into a hole and try as he might, he cannot get out, so he begins to call out for someone to help him. A police officer walks by and the guy yells "hey, officer, can you help me out please"? The officer answers, "sorry buddy, I don't have a rope." Police serve and protect you so unless your life is in danger or you are a danger to the public, they are not going to help.

After a while, a doctor comes along, and the guy yells, "hey can you help me out"? Doc says, I am just a doctor, and I do not have a means of helping, so he writes him a prescription, throws it down the hole and says, "sorry, I can't help but I hope this prescription does." So at least he explained why he could not help, but now, he can say he did something.

Later a friend comes along, and the guy yells "hey, buddy, can you help me out"? The friend politely answers, "I would if I could, but I may get dirty and I don't want to take the risk." Then he asks, "are you thirsty"? And tosses him a bottle of water. The water helps, but again, this is only so he can say he did something.

Finally, his family finds out, looks down the hole at him and the guy says, "I'm glad you came along, now can you help me out"? Family members want to know how this happened; how did he not see the hole? They are aware that in this instance the man fell into the hole due to his negligence, and he needs to figure out how to get himself out of the hole. Truth is, it really does not matter how you got there, you now want out. This is not true of all families.

Then a stranger comes by, sees the guy down in the hole and the guy yells up, "hey buddy, can you help me out"? The stranger jumps down the hole with the guy, and the first guy is stunned. So, he asks, "hey friend, why would you do that? Now we are both stuck down here." The second guy says, "yeah but I've been down here before, and I know the way out."

I am sharing this tale to point out how our experiences can be used to help others. And in this tale the stranger's experience is used as a rescue tool.

How many of us are willing to take a moment to make time and aid someone asking for help? Notice, in this tale, those that could not or were not willing to help, did not even offer to find someone who could help. Help can come in many ways. But it is always guided by the spirit.

Because the man in the hole kept asking for help, - and because, "there's a blessing in your pressing"-, eventually the right person came along to help him in a way which he now, can in turn, use to help someone else, who may be struggling to come out of a hole. You could say the entire event was divinely orchestrated. Of course, the hole represents addiction.

Jesus came to show us the "WAY" and the Holy Spirit remains to continue to light the path. Everyone was born with a light; we just must figure out how and when to use it.

CHAPTER IX

In the previous chapter I related a story about a man who fell into a hole and the events that occurred while he occupied the hole, and later the event that led to him being freed from the hole.

In this chapter of the story, I am going to talk about what happened when he was finally delivered from that predicament.

As I said in the last chapter, the hole is symbolic to the demon of addiction. And though the title refers to someone falling into addiction, in most cases, it was a choice to descend into the trappings of substance abuse.

Now I do have to clear up something. There are those who were drawn into abuse due to being prescribed medication containing opioids to treat an injury. They did not choose to take the path or jump into the hole of abuse. Honestly speaking, you might say they were led to or even pushed into the hole. But they made no effort to climb out. We always have a choice in how we will live.

The demons of addiction cannot make one do their bidding unless one is willing. They try to entice us through our spirit. They search for our weaknesses and exploit them.

Weaknesses that are physical as well as mental. It may well be the case with pharmaceutical companies. These companies often seek to profit from the weaknesses of those who they are supposed to be helping. Their companies may be run by individuals who are possessed, with or without their knowledge. This is an issue for another time.

So, what happened to the guy in the story after he got out of the hole?

From my own experience, overcoming opioid abuse is a process. Getting out of the hole was just the first of many steps. One thing for sure is that demon is still there and is making every effort to keep you under its influence. And this is when the next battle starts.

After getting the physical body free from substance use, the task of freeing the mind comes next, and for many this is the toughest struggle. There are many who have and will relapse, due to their inability to deal with this struggle. That is why the next path or road should lead into a treatment program, which may not eliminate the possibility but can decrease the chance of a relapse. For me, the inpatient program worked best because first, it removed me from situations that might tempt me and second, it made it easier for me to put some distance between me and the period of abuse. This was important because then I began to desire a better lifestyle. One that I could never have imagined while I was in that "hole."

Now, make no mistake, that demon is fully aware that your desires have shifted, and he does not want you to have control over your life. In my case, for years I was controlled by a demonic influence and just like in a divorce from a marriage, where one wants it and the other does not, that demon will try everything to try to win you back. So, how do you combat that? For me it was through prayer and faith in our Creator.

During my time in the treatment center there were instances when Satan would try to cause me to give up and leave before I should have. He tried to detour me. But in every instance, I prayed for strength and guidance and the detours Satan, and his demons tried to use were instantly removed.

1 Peter cha. 5 vs 9 (NIV). *Resist him standing firm in the faith, because you know that the family of believers throughout the world is undergoing the same kind of suffering.*

Recovery is a continuous process and as with life in general there will be some challenges. The challenges of life are a part of life that at times we have no control over. But the challenge of overcoming substance abuse is one battle that once it is fought and won will present new opportunities. Making the next task one of choosing what is the best one and not being afraid to seize it when it occurs. You learn to believe in yourself or as I put it, "Have Faith in Your Faith."

CHAPTER X

On my You Tube channel I talk about the effects and roles demons have in the lives of those who suffer from substance abuse. The examples I gave were based upon my own experiences as a former heroin addict. I talk about how those of us who were abusers were under demonic possession. Videos on this and other abuse related topics can be found on my Overcoming Addiction channel.

My abuse ended over twelve years ago, and since that time I have noticed the continuous growth of opioid use in this country, particularly in low-income communities. Along with this rise there has been an increase in deaths among those who live in these communities. The rise in overdose death from opioids is now being attributed to the addition of the synthetic drugs fentanyl, and a new synthetic known on the street as "tranq."

Illegal drug manufacturers and suppliers now add fentanyl to pot, cocaine, oxycodone, Xanax, and heroin. Just two milligrams of fentanyl would be enough to kill a person.

A lot of the attention goes to celebrities and Caucasian's from suburban areas who are victims of opioid overdoses. But by far the larger number of opioid deaths occur in low-income neighborhoods, where little attention is given unless there are multiple casualties in a brief period. It is in these low-income neighborhoods where Satan has many of his demonic troops. Let me put this in a military context.

Satan is the Commander and Chief of all demons. He commands them to do whatever it takes to keep humanity from exercising dominion over our natural environment. He already has control of the spiritual realm of this planet, and if he could do so, he would have control over both the natural and spiritual. Having control over our own lives would mean that we would have power over him. He was never supposed to have power over humanity.

■■■

How are Satan's Troops Deployed?

He has what could be compared to a military structure. There are Admirals, Generals, Captains, Seargent's, etc. Here is how I would characterize some of their roles.

Satan has his Admirals who in this example, would be someone with the authority to let us say, write legislation and put them into law, which would ensure that these laws would target a specific area of the population. These Admirals would then have their Generals who would then use these laws to target areas like social programs that assist low-income families with things like housing, higher education, health care and unemployment, just to name a few. We will skip the other ranks because their roles are more of one of support. (Judges, police officers, etc.).

Remember these are demons about which I am talking. Not actual individuals who oversee these programs. But anyone who misuses their authority in these types of situations is unknowingly being influenced by demons.

Now we get to the troops. These are the guys that every addict has come in direct contact with. These are the ones who are tasked with finding and introducing us to every unlawful and immoral act there is so we can remain addicted, in effect, destroying our lives. Our interaction with them is through other addicts and suppliers. And it is not surprising that you will find regiments of these demons operating in communities of color across the nation.

Our low-income neighborhoods suffer the most casualties from opioid abuse. Parents with families that are already struggling are taken away from their children, and their spouses because of their addiction, or they become victims of violent crimes committed by someone with a substance abuse problem. And it is not just parents but young adults and little kids who lose their lives because of their own or someone else's addiction. Violence in low-income areas is generated and fueled by substance abuse and it is beginning to spread to other communities. Criminals that were targeting struggling neighborhoods are realizing that high-income areas are more lucrative. These and other crimes are committed by those who are under the influence of demons. And it is my intention to bring attention to this often-hidden enemy.

Ephesians chapter 6 vs 12 states: *for we wrestle not against flesh and blood, but against the rulers, against the authorities, against powers of this dark world, against spiritual forces of evil in heavenly realms.*

When evil spirits take your peace, the goal is not to defeat the evil spirit. The goal is to regain your peace. No individual should hope to defeat an evil spirit. It takes a special anointing to battle demons. The best we can do is recognize them for who they are, seek spiritual guidance, and learn how to resist their influences.

CHAPTER XI:

In the last chapter I talked about the lack of attention given to people of color who suffer and are dying from Opioid Addiction, particularly in African American communities. Addictions of all types are used as tools by spirits, - evil, bad, negative, etc.-, as a means of oppression. Oppression is used to suppress others who may not have access to opportunities of wealth and education. To this point, it is unfortunate that black people living on a continent that contains over 25 % of our global wealth, live in poor underdeveloped nations and in the most deplorable conditions on the planet. Greed and corruption by foreign nations are the main reason Africans are needlessly dying.

Greed is a demonic possession that can have far-reaching influences and consequences. Meaning it will influence brother to harm brother, and neighbor to harm neighbor. Corrupt political leadership has led to starvation, civil wars and genocide among people who are already extremely oppressed. Looking from the outside, it is easy to see how black men in Africa have become easy targets for demons to possess, thus keeping them oppressed. It can be said that oppression and depression is a sign of demonic possession designed to destroy the African race. Satan's goal is to have this same type of destruction happen on a global scale.

■■

Why Are Black People Prime Targets for Demonic Possessions?

This answer might be found in the recounting of the crucifixion of Christ in the Gospels of Matthew, Mark, and Luke. In each of their Gospels they describe an event related to the crucifixion. The symbolism of that event, which was also witnessed by Satan, would have an impact on black men over time.

In the recounting of the crucifixion, there is the mention of an insignificant individual who went by the name of Simon.

■■■

Who Was Simon and What Was His Significance?

Simon was from a Greek city in the province of Cyrenaica located in eastern Libya, in northern Africa. In the Gospels he would be known as Simon of Cyrene. (From Wikipedia).

In Luke's Gospel, chapter 23 vs 26 (NIV) the scripture introduces us to Simon. It reads; *As the soldiers led him away, they seized Simon from Cyrene, who was on his way from the country, and put the cross on him and made him carry it behind Jesus.*

This short mention of that designation by the Roman soldiers to this random individual may have had a profound effect on every black man from that moment on. You see, Simon was a black man. His role as Jesus's cross bearer alerted Satan to the significant role the black man could play in the end times.

Many who study the Bible are aware that Satan made every effort to prevent the birth of Jesus. And because he was unsuccessful, his focus shifted to keeping humanity from recognizing and reacquiring the supernatural authority that was originally given to humanity by our Creator to govern this planet, putting us in control of this natural world that he (Satan) currently rules. Simon helping Jesus bear his cross symbolizes the black man's willingness to help Christians who are struggling to see the same power and authority he witnessed when he looked into the eyes of Jesus. That moment may or may not have changed Simon, but from that moment on, Satan may have decided to make black men his "High Value Targets."

It should be noted that according to the Christian website Aleteia, Simon was a pagan and had been forced to carry the cross. It is not clear whether this had a profound effect on his life at that moment, but some biblical historians believed Simon's heart was touched by grace afterwards. According to the website, Simon initially had no desire to comply with the soldier's command. He may have even felt unlucky at the time. But I believe his presence in the crowd at that precise moment was divinely planned. I point this out because even in our times, sometimes Christians need a little nudge or, as with Simon, need to be divinely placed in a situation where there is no other choice but to obey.

All Christians are expected to pick up the "Cross" for Christ's sake which will happen leading up to the end times.

It was a black man from Africa who was the first to do so, and it could be black men leading the preparation of humanity for the return of Christ. And because of that symbolic act by a man named Simon, Satan is afraid the black men will rally around that symbolism. It is why he spends a great amount of effort targeting black men. It was no accident that the description of Simon was given in the manner it was. So that all would know who he was and where he was from. The argument can still be made that Jesus himself was a man of color but that is a debate that may continue until the end of days. The only thing that should matter is that he was a man sent by our Creator to show us the way to salvation.

I want it to be noted that this is just my opinion of why an entire continent and an entire race of people have been targeted for oppression and suppression. But what is apparent is that Satan fears black people and he is aware of the primary role we could play in the end times.

He believes that if he can keep us oppressed, divided, angry, addicted, fighting among ourselves, and unaware of the real authority we have in this world, he is winning. Those who attempt to "whitewash" and distort the truth the Bible teaches, are under the influence of Satan.

It has been argued that black people are the true "Chosen People" mentioned in the book of Genesis. And if so, Satan will launch every demonic attack he has against us. He does not know when it will happen or who will be the one or ones to rise and lead the way in preparing humanity for the return of Christ, so he attacks us all. This is why we must arm ourselves in preparation for spiritual attacks by demonic forces. Will we rise to the challenge?

CHAPTER XII

Demonic possessions can affect every aspect of life. They affect our minds through their influences. Our minds are where we first encounter demonic disruptions. They affect our emotions, thoughts, and actions. Acts of violence, lust, and dishonesty are evidence of demonic possession. These acts originate as thoughts that gain access to our spirit through our minds. Our hearing and eyesight can be utilized by demonic spirits as portals or gateways into our minds and our souls.

It is through these senses (hearing and sight), that a demon will look for a weakness to exploit. Once they find a weak area, they will use it to gain access to and disrupt other areas of our lives. For example: if someone has a weakness for alcohol, that weakness provides an opening for a demon to enter and attempt to tear down one's resistance in other areas. This will allow things like violence and lust to grow, which are actions that the demon will influence us to act upon. Once a demon influences one area of life it will try to influence other areas. Their desire is to be completely satisfied, which can only be achieved using our minds and bodies. If one cannot do damage alone, it calls on other demons to help. For a substance abuser it is important to resist, or "barricade" oneself from them when they first attempt to enter our minds, since they are the promoters of all addictions.

■■

Constructing Barriers

There is no one way of protecting against demonic possessions, it takes layers of protection. In my experience as a former substance abuser, I found that a barrier must be built to keep demons from taking possession of our lives. Anyone who is already under one's influence must first seek to repel it before a protective barrier can be built. Once a demon has taken possession it is hard to dispose of. The longer one is kept around, the harder it will be to get rid of it, (like an addiction). Because demons are supernatural beings, resisting and repelling them will require supernatural assistance.

To repel a demon will require two elements. The first is Prayer.

The initiation of prayer is the foundation to build on. The construction of anything begins with a foundation. Prayer petitions our Creator to act on our behalf in all situations. It should always be the first act.

The second element is Recognition of Authority. We as human beings must recognize who we are and the authority we have over demons. The only way outside influences can affect us is if we allow them to and this occurs when we do not have a barrier in place (resistance). Once a person meets a demonic spirit, the ability to resist becomes the first barrier it will seek to tear down.

It requires willpower to maintain a barrier. Demons are uncomfortable confronting willpower. Willpower is what has been taken away from an addict so when a demon sees one gaining it back, it will attack that person relentlessly.

Every Christian knows that in the beginning, humanity was given dominion over this planet and its products. Demons want to take pleasures in the natural world as they once did before God turned dominion of the natural world over to humanity, which is why they need our mind and bodies. They will destroy all of humanity just for their pleasure. Greed, oppression, and abuse of power are other demonic possessions. For someone under the influence of substances, the continuous practice of prayer and exercising the authority given by the Creator is a requirement needed to repel demonic possessions. Only then can the process of building a barrier begin for them. Simply put, if you think you need treatment, get it!

∎∎

Tools of Construction

We can find tools for building a barrier against demons in the book of Ephesians. Chapter 6. Starting at verse 10, from the NIV. *Finally, be strong in the Lord and in His mighty power. Vs. 10 Put on the full armor of God so that you can take your stand against the devil's schemes. Vs. 12 for our struggle is not against flesh and blood but against the rulers against authorities against the powers of this dark world and against the spiritual forces of evil in the heavenly realms*

Also in this chapter, it talks about the belt of truth buckled around your waist. The breastplate of righteousness in place. Your feet are fitted with readiness that comes from the gospel of peace. The shield of faith which can extinguish all flaming arrows of the evil one. The helmet of salvation and the sword of the Spirit which is the word of God. These "tools" should be used to guard against demons, with the "Shield of Faith" being the one I use the most.

Again, the foundation should always be prayer. Prayer gives us the wisdom and knowledge we need to effectively use these and other powerful tools against demons.

Donning the "Breastplate of Righteousness" indicates to God that our prayers are from the heart. From this chapter in the book of Ephesians alone we are given basic tools to build the first layers of resistance or barriers for our protection and instructions on how to use them against demons.

Our brains are biologically engineered to be a gateway. Information, thoughts, and ideas use this gateway. Demons also seek to hide themselves in these areas to gain access. The "Helmet of Salvation" is designed to be used as a barrier to prevent their access. The "Full Armor of God" will provide a basic layer of protection against demons. Using this basic principle will generate additional layers of protection when needed. I am not going into many details because I want those reading this to open this chapter in the book of Ephesians and interpret how the "Armor of God" can help protect you.

■■■

Guard Your Entry Ports

Social, print, electronic and mainstream media are "gold mines" for demons. Through these mediums demons can conduct their relentless efforts to influence us. Also, this is where they use coercion, deception, misinformation, false narratives, perversion, and other bad traits to gain access to our minds. Their influences can be seen in movies, on television and in music. Our eyes and ears are primary ports of entry that they can use. We must be careful of what we read, watch, and listen to, especially our youth. It is important that they are taught to develop a strong will, which will empower them against the demonic forces that target them constantly.

There is no one fits all forms of protection against Satan and his demonic forces. It must be built to accommodate the individual. But a barrier built using the basics found in the book of Ephesians will generate protection against all demons. Because of our prior weakness, recovering addicts need a highly effective wall of protection. If anyone is attempting to regain their willpower, reach out for help. Regaining willpower shows the effort being made towards recovery. Satan deploys demons whose only assignment is to tear down willpower and open ports.

CHAPTER XIII

M any of us who follow the teachings in the Bible know the benefits of prayer and meditation. It is the action of asking a question or asking for directions from our Creator and hearing his response.

Taken from the Book of Matthews, Chapter 7, verse seven through eight, the scripture reads; *ask and it shall be given you. Seek and you shall find; knock and it shall be open unto you. Vs. 8. For everyone that Asks; receives, and he that seeks it, finds it, and to him that knock, it shall be open.*

I am going to share a story of a man or a (person). who because of his desire to find and understand truth, was led to an encounter with our Creator. I am not going to name this individual, but for those who have studied the Bible, the identity will become evident, but I will reveal his identity towards the end of this chapter.

Since I am telling this story, I get to tell it in my own way. It begins in a small village where a young boy is working in his father's small shop. The father was the idol maker for the village. The people of this village worshiped many different gods, just as the boy's father did. Most of his carvings were made from wood, which allowed the man to make them very quickly. And he made them in many sizes.

One afternoon while alone in his father's shed, one of the larger idols fell over and the head broke off from its body. Now the boy had been curious as to what kind of power these gods possessed. So, when the idol fell, he asked himself; why the god do not repair himself? The boy tried to upright the idol, but it was too heavy for him, so he called for his father to help. Rather than struggling to lift it back into place, the father decided to destroy the idol but keep the head to use it on another idol. This seemed odd to the boy because people worshiped these idols as being powerful, and yet this one had fallen, lost its head, and could not get up on its own. The young boy began to question the power of these gods his father was producing.

That evening, the father ordered his son to prepare a fire to cook their dinner. He instructed the lad to use the splintered wood from the fallen idol. As he was doing so, he found a small idol among some other discarded pieces of wood and decided to leave this little god in charge of tending to the fire so it would not burn out while he was away preparing the meal to be cooked. When he returned, he saw that the god which he left to tend the fire had itself begun to burn. Very soon it became consumed by the fire, and the young boy laughed to himself and said, "the gods my father has made of wood are easily consumed by the fire". "Maybe the fire is the more powerful god". After the dinner was cooked, the father ordered his son to put the fire out as it was still burning. As he did so, he thought to himself, water can put out a fire, then water is the more powerful god. Notice, he never mentions his concerns to his father about their power or lack thereof. Because there were things he did not yet understand, he believed his father would not take too kindly to being questioned by a child over these things. But unknowingly to him, there was someone who was paying attention to his inquiries.

In those days, there were no geological surveys or scientific data for the boy to study that would show the proportions of land and water on our planet. All he knew was what he saw, but he did have the understanding that water was on the earth, and because of this he determined that the earth must be the more powerful god because it holds up the water.

After believing this for a while, he notices that sunlight has the power to grow things on the earth, such as materials for food and housing, as well as provide light and warmth. So, he says to himself, then the sun must be the more powerful god because it is the source of sunlight. Then he realized that every day the sunlight is overrun by darkness. And if the darkness can do that to the light from the sun, then it must be the more powerful god. The young man never stopped seeking to understand the world around him. And it is because he never stopped, our Creator decided to show the young man the truth in what he is seeking, which unbeknownst to him was the source of everything. In other words, the young lad by now was seeking the Almighty God.

As the young lad was sitting alone one day and pondering his latest idea of who is the more powerful God, He heard a thundering voice called out to him. Though he saw no one around, the boy answered, " I am here", and the voice said, "I am the God you seek". Now I am sure this response caused some fear in the young man because it was a thundering voice that he heard in his mind. -When our God wants our attention, He will leave no doubt as to who He is speaking.

 Now the first thing God does when he contacts us is give us the reason he is doing so. And it is because he has a particular purpose for us or- as was the case in this story, because we are seeking something from him. And sometimes before we can receive what we ask for, he will give us a task to perform. Often- as was the ways detailed in the Old Testament of the bible, the task may be in the form of a sacrifice. These actions serve two purposes, first, to demonstrate our obedience, and 2nd to show us that He is who He says He is. In the case of the young man, God required a sacrifice which the young man was eager to do. God rewards our eagerness to seek him, and in this case, he rewarded the young man by appearing before him after his sacrifice.

From the time he was a young boy, he had questions and wanted a better understanding of why he often felt uneasy going to the market to sell the idols his father had made, and now, as a young man, he gets to have a face to face with God.

God showed him how everything came into existence, including how the beginning of humanity was discussed among He and what I call, "his board of trusted spirits". He saw early on that the young man was determined to know the truth.

■■■

Identity Revealed

If you have not already figured out who this young man in the story is, he grew to become the one our God decided to make the father of many nations The one God would call, Abraham.

Matthew Chapter 6, verse 33. (KJV) But seek you first, the Kingdom of God and his righteousness, and all these things will be added unto you. The scripture did not say some things, but all things. Abraham started as a child seeking a better understanding of what he saw around him.

 The false gods his father built obviously had no power. He felt a god should be all powerful-or at least have some power, and in his father's idols he saw no power, and yet people worship them. This bothered him, and he sought answers as to why. When a righteous person is diligently seeking answers, God gives them to him. Abraham was given the wisdom and understanding of who God is because he believed a God should be all powerful. So, he sought wisdom and understanding which is given by our Creator to all that seek it. God is the source. Abraham was rewarded with being named by God as the father of many nations. These were the things that were added to him because he diligently sought "Kingdom Knowledge".

There is an especially important event to note in this story. Abraham was required to do something that was necessary before he could accomplish everything God had planned for his life.

In the book of Genesis, chapter 12 vs 2 (KJV) we see where the Lord said to Abram, *"I will make you into a great nation, and I will bless you. I will make your name great, and you will be a blessing. Verse 3. "I will bless those who bless you, and whoever curses you, I will curse, and all people on earth will be blessed through you."*

But in Genesis 12 Verse 1 (KJV) we see what the Lord said to Abram, *"go from your country, your people and your father's house to the land I will show you".*

Before the Lord would do that which he had promised to Abram he first had to leave his father's house. Abram could no longer be in his father's presence because his father built and worshiped false gods. The Lord knew that the evil spirits connected to Abrams's father because of his idol worship, would try to connect and continuously try to influence Abram because he sought truth. Evil spirits do not want us to know the truth which comes when we have a relationship with our Lord and Savior. (There is a much better life promised to the one struggling with addiction after leaving the "House" where addiction dwells).

There may be times when we are hesitant to ask questions regarding things that make us uncomfortable. One should never be afraid to seek an understanding of something in any situation. Especially if it will directly impact your life. Be it at work, in a relationship, in our churches and especially when struggling with abuse of any kind. All these areas have a direct impact on our life.

Although I told this story in my own way the message is clear. We should always ask questions. We should seek to understand until we understand. Understanding what we are talking about to others allows them to understand us. I am still getting answers to questions I may have asked days, months or even years ago.

God answers all inquiries of the righteous. If not directly, then he will guide you to the answer. If you seek him first.

I have a saying, having" a clear understanding will help you to be clearly understood." To spread the Gospel, you must do so where people can clearly understand it. It is the same with reaching out to help someone struggling with any abuse.

CHAPTER XIV:

M editation is a helpful tool that can be used in many ways. It can be used to induce relaxation through the relief from anxieties that many substance abusers frequently experience. Anxieties that not only occur during the struggle, but very often occur during the treatment process and afterwards. So, what is the definition of meditation?

According to Wikipedia, *"meditation is a practice in which an individual uses a technique -such as mindfulness, or focusing the mind on a particular object, thought, or activity -to train attention and awareness and achieve a mentally clear and emotionally calm and stable state."*

I began using meditation long before I overcame my addiction. It was easier to do when I was medicated than it was when I had no drugs in my system. What meditation did at that time was make me aware of the maddening lifestyle I was living. I began to become more aware and pay more attention to my co-workers and my family's perception of me (all my friends at the time were substance abusers as well so it did not matter what they thought). Even though there was no immediate action on my part to change, I was more conscious of how I was received. What humbled me more was that they never treated me with degradation or disdain. The more I meditated, the more I began to want to change.

Meditation requires focus, commitment, dedication, and practice. And as an addict, I was unable to maintain these requirements, but I kept trying and even though I was not doing it as much as I should have, I might not be here today if I had not spent any time meditating back then. Today I made meditation a part of my daily routine. It helps me to relax so I can clear my mind and focus on the clarity and understanding that I seek.

As of this date I am 12 ½ years substance free and there are still moments of stress I experience from time to time. These instants may at times cause some pressure but that's part of everyday life. As a recovering addict I can honestly say that not having a dependency is one less pressure with which I must cope. It is through meditation that I can easily deal with the emotions and pressures that accompany stress.

Daily Meditation Will Strengthen You Against Demonic Influences

In the definition of meditation, there is a phrase "focusing the mind on a particular object, thought or activity." Most of what I am going to describe next is based upon my individual experiences.

As I said, I use meditation to relax and clear my mind. The primary reason for me doing so is to have a clear and uninterrupted connection with my Creator. Having a clear and uninterrupted connection allows a continuous flow of inspiration and revelations which all artists, writers, or anyone suffering from an affliction need. Meditation also provides me with supernatural conformation of natural information.

Much of what we read and hear is subject to contamination by unseen forces. For me meditation gives me the ability to see through much of the misinformation that those who are under the influence of demonic forces would have us believe. With that being said, I have discovered that Satan is aware of my growing capabilities and has some clever ways to distract me. He constantly tries to keep me from connecting with my "Source" because the more I connect with it, the more deceptions I can recognize. Recognizing demons and their deceptions is a powerful weapon against them. A strong-willed individual deters demons.

Sometimes when I am meditating, and I am not focusing on a particular subject, I just ask to be shown whatever it is I need to see or understand. When I do so, many times I just get peace of mind. But there are times when a stream of thought begins, and I wind up with an article to share or a theme for my podcast. In many cases I wind up with a chapter for an upcoming book. Like this one for instance. Then there are some streams that reveal the actions of people, like those of government institutions, judicial institutions and for me the most irritating institution of them all, TV ads. Sometimes I can see the deception used to influence people to purchase products that benefits the sellers and advertisers more than it does the consumers. During these non-specific meditations is when Satan tries to distract me the most.

Let me share an example of one of Satan's tricks that I experienced. One morning, immediately after my non-specific supplication, I envisioned myself walking down some stairs. I realized that I was taking someone down with me who I determined was one of Satan's demons. My first thought was, I am taking this demon down where it will not do me or anyone else harm. It was not until I looked at its face that I saw it was smiling at me. That is when I realized that I was not taking it down, it was taking me down. It was distracting me from what I should have been doing and that was connecting and listening to my "Source."

What the enemy was doing with me was causing me to spend time disengaging with him instead of engaging with my Creator. The more time I spend scuffling with his demons means less time I hear from the Holy Spirit. My solution: whenever I spend time disengaging from Satan and his demons, it is time I can use to familiarize myself with them so I can better identify them. The sooner I can identify them the sooner I can dismiss them.

For a person overcoming substance abuse it is particularly important to build a strong connection with our Creator. A connection of this type can work as a barrier against the pressures that everyone faces. Strengthening my connection prepared me for the many temptations that Satan still tries to use against me.

Unlike those who have never struggled with addiction for a length of time, recovering addicts have a lot of baggage or skeletons. Many times, while I am meditating, Satan will interrupt my thoughts and attempt to show me my many past activities that even as an addict, I enjoyed indulging in.

So, if I am meditating on something, and for a fraction of an instant I get distracted or interrupted, that is the moment when he reminds me of all the various forms of entertainment that excite me during those years of substance abuse. The less baggage a person has, the less likely it is that it can be used as a form of temptation or condemnation. Temptation can cause anxiety.

Condemnation can generate guilt; both can cause pressure that leads to stress.

Meditation is always my first step towards addressing all my situations, good and bad. The wonderful thing now is that there are fewer dreadful things to meditate on and more good things to be grateful for. Meditation should always be preceded by prayer. Whenever I pray for something, I always expect an answer or a solution. It may not be right away, and it may not be what I want to hear, but a determination is always made. Usually, when there is no immediate answer, it is my dedication and determination being evaluated.

Every chapter in this book is dedicated to recognizing and coping with the pressures that surround addiction. But the methods demonstrated in these chapters can be applied to any form of affliction or abuse.

By sharing some of my experiences I hope to help others identify and confront the source of all abuses which are demonic possessions. Demons are everywhere and they look to affect us in every way possible. It is up to us to make their possessions less of a possibility.

Prayers and Meditation helped me, and I know it will help whoever is reading this.

James 5:16 *Confess your faults one to another, and pray for one another, that ye may be healed. The effectual fervent prayer of the righteous availeth much.* From the King James NIV version.

Be on the lookout for the next publication from me. The book is called," A Revolution Against Satan and His

Demons." It will give some details on how we can revolt against Satan's governmental system.

About *the* Author

S.R. Mays was born in Chicago, Illinois, in 1956. His mother had him at a very young age, so he practically lived with his godparents while his mom finished school.

Mays had a simple upbringing throughout grammar school. By the time he reached high school, he had nine siblings. It was in his first year of high school when his father passed away, and at that moment, life for him would be altered. Mays was the oldest, so I was counted on to help with his younger sisters and brothers. During his second year of high school, he started drinking alcohol before and after school.

Mays was trying to change his perception of the situation. He had begun to feel that he wasn't having enough fun as a teenager. By his senior year in high school, he drank and smoked pot. A year after his graduation in 1974, he was introduced to heroin. Soon he began experimenting with other substances.

In 1976 Mays became a father for the first time. He also started his first real job at a printing company that year. In 1979 he married for the first and only time, and in 1982 his second child was born. By 1985 the marriage had ended. And by 1987, when the printing company closed, May's substance abuse intensified. Also, in 1987 he met someone, and in 1988 his third child was born. He continued to struggle with substance abuse until 2011. Since then, Mays has remained substance abuse-free, thanks to hard work and the support of his mother Margaret and his siblings Saundra, and Catherine, the twins Sharon and Shelly, Rhonda and her twin Rondale, Kenneth, and his half-brother Bobby.

Mays greatest motivation came from his two oldest children, Ray and Trinette, who have remained constant with their motivation and support. And most importantly, he gives thanks to the Creator. The Creator gave him his family; without them, he could not have survived the thirty-plus years of substance abuse.

Currently, Mays time is spent motivating others through the lessons he has learned over those thirty-plus years. His days are filled with thinking of ways to help our youth and young adults through some of life's struggles using the tools he writes about in this book. Mays tries to be a better person each day than he was the day before. He always tells people he's grateful to wake up each day, and everything after he wakes up is a bonus.

Introducing a very grateful and humble servant, **S. R. Mays**

www.ingramcontent.com/pod-product-compliance
Lightning Source LLC
Chambersburg PA
CBHW021653120626
46545CB00002B/837